APPRECIATION FOR
GRANTSMANSHIP: PROGRAM PLANNING & PROPOSAL WRITING

All grant proposal writers will benefit from Grantsmanship: Program Planning & Proposal Writing, *with its essential framework for success. I've used this model for nearly 35 years— as a Grantsmanship Center trainer, a grantseeker, and a grantmaker. Norton Kiritz showed the way and this new edition is beautifully illustrated, clearly edited, and a page-turner to boot. Go turn it into money!*

JENNIFER LEONARD
President and CEO
Rochester Area Community Foundation (NY)

I learned all that I needed to know about grants and grant proposal writing from The Grantsmanship Center. From their classes to this updated book, you'll find all the answers you need for writing a winning proposal.

CHRISTINE PIVEN, Ph.D.
Chief of Staff, Community & Culture
Office of the Managing Director, City of Philadelphia

As a government administrator who provides capacity-building training and resource technical assistance to community-based organizations, this model is my 'bible' for helping nonprofits secure grant funding. I waited impatiently for this new version and I'm so glad it's here! It keeps the best of the original and it's even more relevant for today's ever-changing and challenging environments.

STEPHEN D. CLARK
Senior Management Analyst
U.S. Department of Housing and Urban Development

Grantsmanship: Program Planning & Proposal Writing *is the required text in my upper level Grant Proposal Writing course. It's an invaluable tool for college students from the thought leaders in the field.*

BERNARD TURNER, Ed.D., GPC
Associate Professor of Social Entrepreneurship
Belmont University

Grantsmanship: Program Planning & Proposal Writing *takes you through every stage of the process—from conceptualization to writing plainly. It's an essential companion for any serious fundraiser. Don't buy one... buy two... and give a copy to someone who's struggling to raise funds. It will be a gift that will repay many, many times.*

BERNARD ROSS
Director
The Management Centre

This book is an indispensable resource for even the most accidental of grant proposal writers. It acknowledges the importance of connecting organizational planning and proposal writing, and it is plain-spoken and elegantly written—clarifying the practice while bringing it down to earth. But what I most appreciate is that it integrates a treasure trove of how-to's into an unflinchingly moral framework that places consulting with the nonprofit's constituents as the first step in the right way to ask for money.

RUTH McCAMBRIDGE
President and Editor in Chief
Nonprofit Quarterly

There are scores of guides on grant proposal writing, but none that provide such thorough and practical help. No book can guarantee that you'll get the grant, but this book will dramatically improve your chances for success.

JOEL J. OROSZ
Former Program Director, W.K. Kellogg Foundation;
Author of The Insider's Guide to Grantmaking

Grantsmanship: Program Planning & Proposal Writing, *has been my go-to grant resource for years. No one else provides as comprehensive and strategic an approach to supporting carefully planned programs with a well-crafted grant proposal. With this latest edition, which has been thoughtfully updated and expanded to reflect today's grant seeking and grant making landscape, Norton Kiritz's work will continue to serve as the must-read, grant-related guide for years to come.*

HAL COHEN
Secretary
Vermont Agency of Human Services

The main word that comes to mind with this book is "useful." Useful is all we need and something we rarely find. The layout and the language are easy to follow and easy to read, yet convey a wealth of helpful information and excellent examples. Thank you for updating this treasure and making it available to another generation of grantseekers.

KIM KLEIN
Author of Fundraising for Social Change

People love this book because it's like rocket fuel for great program planning and proposal writing. When we sponsor The Grantsmanship Center's workshops for Missouri nonprofits to learn how to design outcome-focused programs, every participant gets a copy of this mind-changing book. We also give away copies to colleagues at other organizations knowing that, like Johnny Chapman did with his apple seeds, the more you spread something good, the more good will sprout.

MICHAEL RENNER
Program Officer
Missouri Foundation for Health

What a pleasure to read the same crisp, concise writing that was the hallmark of Norton Kiritz's original efforts. The book is ethical, easy to understand and shot-through with optimism. Grantsmanship *is an empowering piece that reminds us that there is no mystery to obtaining grants for our organization, just clear-headed logic and determination. Thank you for a wonderful read.*

JACK SHAKELY
President Emeritus
California Community Foundation

Grantsmanship:
Program Planning & Proposal Writing

Norton J. Kiritz

Updated and expanded by Barbara Floersch

Edited by Cathleen E. Kiritz

Grantsmanship: Program Planning & Proposal Writing
Second Edition, second printing

Published by
The Grantsmanship Center, Los Angeles, CA 90017 USA
www.tgci.com

Library of Congress Cataloging-Publication Data
Kiritz, Norton J., 1935 — 2006
Floersch, Barbara, 1950 —
Grantsmanship: Program Planning & Proposal Writing / Norton J. Kiritz;
Updated and expanded by Barbara Floersch
Edited by Cathleen E. Kiritz

Includes index.
1. Grantsmanship   2. Funding   3. Title

© Copyright 1974-2017 The Grantsmanship Center. All rights reserved.
ISBN 978-1-930250-03-1

Library of Congress Control Number: 2017949075

Photo Credits
James Carroll, pages: 54, 73, 103, 127, 134,147

Marshall Clarke, pages: 21, 22, 34, 46, 48, 74, 78, 97, 110, 131, 175, 215

Cathleen Elliott Kiritz, page 215

Anna Kaufman Moon, pages: 38, 58

Jonathan Moore, page: 76

United American Indian Involvement (UAII), page xii

Western Education Association, page: 12

Designed by
BravoCharlieTango and Brand Navigation

Printed by
Monarch Litho, Inc., Montebello, CA

The people, places and situations used in the examples in this book are fictitious. They have been created to make specific points and any resemblance to actual people or organizations is coincidental.

Grantsmanship:
Program Planning & Proposal Writing

Contents

Acknowledgements

This book is in your hands because we had help and support from many people.

It would never have been completed without the patience and steadfast commitment of Alex Kiritz and Larry Floersch.

Our heartfelt thanks also go to Jim Abernathy, Susan Andres, Sandy Banks, Christine Black, Ernest Black, Thomas R. Blackburn, Linda Boedeker, Tom Boyd, Gail Brauner, Bresee Foundation, Edna Brown, Susan Chandler, Bill Chiaravalle, Marshall Clarke, Mary Ruth Clowdsley, Color Inc., Mark Eiduson, Pablo Eisenberg, Hadrian Floersch, Nick & Melissa Floersch, Henry Flood, Debra Gadsby, Bradley & Ida Gardner, Ella Gardner, Judy Gooch, Noel Greenwood, Dan Hally, Patty Hasselbring, Tom Howard, Ron Jacobs, Matt Keener, Sarah Kim, AJ King, Nicholas Kiritz, Dorothy Elliott Lasher, Christine Lavery, Leslie Memsic, M.D., Keith Monley, Ericka Novotny, Alvertha Penny, Claudia & William Perozzi, Chuck & Linda Putney, David Rambeau, Matthew Reichman, Angela Richardson, Dorothy Watson Smith, Roger Stephenson, Blake & Allison Tannery, Kevin Wiberg, and William Zinsser.

Thank you also to the more than a million people who have read, used, and cherished the original *Program Planning & Proposal Writing* and who have helped to inspire this work.

Support for the update of *Program Planning & Proposal Writing* was generously provided by the Annenberg Foundation and the California Community Foundation.

Foreword

Norton Kiritz, founder of The Grantsmanship Center, was a passionate supporter of nonprofit organizations, a believer in their capacity to do good, and an astute critic of a philanthropic community that made life difficult for many charitable groups.

His work with social service organizations convinced him that nonprofits had to become more skilled in the art of grantsmanship. So Norton established The Grantsmanship Center to help nonprofits do just that—improve their program planning, write stronger proposals, and hone evaluation skills, all critical ingredients for securing foundation and government funds to support their missions and programs. His simply written, clear guide, *Program Planning & Proposal Writing*, changed how grantseekers and grantmakers approach their work.

In my view, this widely celebrated publication remains, after 40 years, the best handbook about how to win grants. It is also a tool that brings focus to the essential elements of operating a successful organization. It neither preaches nor sets arbitrary standards. What it does is advise nonprofits to follow a logical approach in developing their goals, objectives, plans, and funding strategies.

This guide has had an enormous impact in the U.S. and is used in over 40 countries throughout the world. It has positively changed the direction and effectiveness of countless organizations and has been translated into Chinese, Spanish, and Ukrainian.

To meet the needs of a changing nonprofit sector, The Grantsmanship Center has now issued an updated and expanded version of *Program Planning & Proposal Writing*. This expertly revised new edition retains the essence of Norton's work while adding new information, stories, and examples that make it more relevant to today's reader.

Now titled *Grantsmanship: Program Planning & Proposal Writing*, this publication is a worthy successor to the original guide. It is the most thorough, perceptive, and practical guide to grant proposal writing that we are likely to have for years to come.

PABLO EISENBERG

Senior Fellow, *McCourt School of Public Policy, Georgetown University*
Columnist, *Chronicle of Philanthropy*
Columnist, *Huffington Post*

Impact

United American Indian Involvement (UAII) got its start on Los Angeles' Skid Row almost 40 years ago. Now it's the largest urban Native American nonprofit in the United States, bringing medical care, mental health treatment, youth services, and education to thousands of Native Americans in Southern and Central California.

Its programs are effective and its positive impact on lives is concrete. A diabetic grandmother learns to exercise and cook healthy meals. A homeless veteran gets the counseling he needs to find stability. Children in tough neighborhoods are pointed toward college through enrichment activities.

UAII is an example of how hard work and dedication have made one organization a leader in its field and an effective champion for the community it serves. And it is also one example of how a group of committed people have used The Grantsmanship Center's *Program Planning & Proposal Writing* approach to help achieve its mission.

"We had five employees, a $300,000 budget, and a tiny office on Skid Row," recalled UAII Executive Director Dave Rambeau, who rallied a small group of like-minded people in 1979 to tackle the daunting problems confronting urban Indians. "We needed money to keep the programs going and to expand to meet other needs."

None of the staff had the expertise to grow funding for the agency. "So we went to this Indian guy at UCLA," Rambeau said, "and he recommended Norton Kiritz and The Grantsmanship Center. He said that was the place to start if you're looking to learn."

That referral was the beginning of a long relationship between UAII and the Center. "I took the training and started applying for money," Rambeau said. His first proposal generated a $25,000 grant from Los Angeles County, giving his group the confidence and credibility to tap other funding sources.

"What we learned from Norton helped raise our profile, and that allowed us to get more funding," Rambeau said. The *Program Planning & Proposal Writing* approach was Rambeau's blueprint for documenting and articulating the case for funding and for developing logical and realistic program plans. "I'd go back to Norton for help whenever I got stuck," said Rambeau. He continues to send his staff to The Grantsmanship Center for training. And since it began using the Center's model, UAII has expanded to three cities, with more than 130 employees and an annual budget of $8.5 million.

But grant dollars are only a means to an end, and the true measure of success is impact. UAII's grant funding is well-targeted and well-spent. It contributes toward the organization's mission in a way that transforms lives and will pay dividends for generations to come.

You can see the impact of the agency's growth in its annual Robert Sundance Summer Youth Camp. The camp started with eight kids on Skid Row and now takes 150 Native American children from Central and Southern California to the High Sierra every summer to fish, swim, bike, ride horses, climb rocks, and careen down ziplines.

But it's more than just a good time. Campers get physical exams, healthy food, and real-life guidance. The rules are strict—no video games, cellphones, or music players—and social support follows the campers home. Family services and school-year activities help these children from tough, discouraging circumstances to blossom and become leaders. Many of them even go back to camp as counselors, dedicated to helping young children succeed as they did.

To this day, UAII uses the principles of grantsmanship laid out in this book, strengthening its ability to attract the funding it needs to continue to serve and fortify its community.

SANDY BANKS

Columnist, *Los Angeles Times*

Grantsmanship:
Program Planning & Proposal Writing

What Is Grantsmanship?

Grantsmanship is a philosophy, a code of ethics, and a set of skills that, when practiced together, can produce positive change. Here's how The Grantsmanship Center defines it.

When you practice grantsmanship:

- You never lose sight of your organization's mission.

- You know your field and stay up to date on relevant research and best practices.

- You know the people and the community your organization serves and treat them with genuine respect, encouraging their input and involvement.

- You're committed to planning because you know it's essential to making a real difference.

- You engage others in planning—staff, constituents, board members, community members, other organizations—because you value diverse perspectives.

- You build partnerships with colleague organizations, not because the funders say you have to, but because you're committed to the expanded viewpoints, resources, and program effectiveness that genuine partnerships bring.

- You view funders as partners, allies, advisors, and advocates.

- You proactively search for funding opportunities that fit your organization's mission and priorities rather than passively waiting for something "right" to come along.

- You refuse to misrepresent or fabricate information, disparage other organizations, or compromise a program in order to win a grant.

A grant is not about money alone, because money by itself doesn't protect battered families, help children to read, fill the plates of the hungry, clean polluted lakes, or open museum doors. But when a grant is used to finance a well-planned program run by a capable and committed organization, it can be a powerful catalyst for change. A grant is a tool—a means to an end.

Similarly, the size of a grant is not the measure of success. A large grant to support an ill-conceived program can be a waste of money. A small grant to support a well-designed program can be tremendously effective. Grantsmanship is not about chasing dollars—it's about getting good results.

In language,
clarity is everything.

CONFUCIOUS

Getting Started
You're Not Alone

You've got a great idea or an important project in mind—something your organization can do to make the world better. Now what? How can you transform these good intentions into effective action? No matter what's motivating you, the next step is to answer some questions. Why is the work necessary? What is the change you want to see? How can your organization make it happen? Where should you start? And at some point, what will it cost and where will the money come from?

This book is here to help. It lays out The Grantsmanship Center Model for planning programs and then writing grant proposals to fund them.

Originated by Norton J. Kiritz in 1972, this model is the accepted standard in the field. It has been adopted throughout the world by grantmakers to establish grant proposal guidelines and by grantseekers to write grant proposals.

Always start with planning. Imagine a complex road trip without a map, a clock, or a GPS. A program and a grant proposal that aren't based on good planning have the same disadvantages. They're likely to be off track, unlikely to inspire confidence or support, and most important, less likely to generate good results.

A program plan must be able to withstand a hard shake because those who award grant funds will do just that—give your grant proposal a tough examination. You must be able to explain your concern, the desired changes, what your organization wants to do, how you'll measure change, how you'll sustain the work beyond grant funding, and how your organization will spend the requested money.

Good, solid planning is the foundation for success. Once a plan is in place, you're prepared to speak intelligently on the topic, to rally community support, to build partnerships, to influence decision makers, and to write compelling grant proposals. You're ready to make the case for support.

Organizations that devote sufficient time and energy to the planning process can reap benefits beyond grant funding. These often include:

- increased understanding of the problem
- clarity about long-term goals
- a focus on measurable program outcomes
- better program evaluations
- better record-keeping systems
- more targeted use of resources and better financial management
- enhanced credibility.

Using This Model for Planning

Effective program planning can't be done in a vacuum, sitting alone in a corner, separate from the views of others. Involve board members, administrators, those who will run the program, and most important, the beneficiaries.

Welcoming others from outside your organization into the process will bring fresh perspectives that aren't available in-house. Tap the expertise of collaborating organizations and community experts.

When developing a grant proposal, it's essential to allow adequate time for both planning and writing. Clear writing can't compensate for an incoherent plan.

The Grantsmanship Center Model includes eight categories or sections of information, which are discussed beginning on page 13. Of those eight sections, three are particularly important because they make up the core of the proposal: Problem, Outcomes, and Methods. By involving others as you answer questions raised in these sections, your organization will strengthen its plan and give it a better chance of success.

First examine the problem. Start by exploring the situation that's motivating your organization to take action—what we call the problem. Use this book's discussion of the problem as a planning guide to help you formulate the questions to be answered

and identify data you'll need to gather and decipher.

It can take time to develop a full understanding of the situation. You may need to convene meetings, talk to people who are affected, conduct online research, read reports, and talk to experts. But this is time well spent. Until you understand the situation, its significance, and its causes, it's not possible to propose a solution.

Determine what change is possible. Once you understand the problem, you're ready to consider how you want that situation to change—what we call outcomes. For example, if the concern is the poor reading scores of students, the planning team will consider how much improvement you should aim for. Use this book's discussion of outcomes to guide your planning.

Decide how your organization will produce the desired change. When considering how much change is reasonable to expect, your planning team will naturally start thinking about what approaches can produce the change—what we call the methods. Use this book's discussion of methods to guide your planning.

It can be tempting to start the planning process by considering the methods your organization wishes to implement. Please don't. To produce change, the methods must relate directly to the cause of the problem. So until you've defined the problem and have an understanding of why it exists, you're not in a position to propose an approach for correcting it.

The Grantsmanship Center Model isn't a magic formula. It's just an orderly way of organizing your thinking as you plan a program or an activity. Use this format to develop your plan. Then draw from the plan what's needed for any specific grant application.

This format is primarily for program grants. Modifications are required in proposals for arts and culture, capital projects, strengthening agency infrastructure, general operating support, planning, or research. In the last chapter you'll find guidance on adapting this model for these other types of proposals. Since this model is the basic recipe upon which all variations are based, it's important to understand it first.

Some Basics

Who should write a grant proposal?
Some organizations have a full-time "grants coordinator," "director of development," "planning director," "federal aid specialist," or the like. But most proposals are developed by a staff person who wears another hat (or two or three). Because planning and proposal writing are so tightly related, whoever writes the proposal should have access to the organization's decision-makers.

Whether working independently or as the head of a team, the lead proposal developer needs to act as a facilitator, bringing the concerns of the beneficiaries, the applicant organization, and the funding source into one coherent and logical plan. To do this well requires a high level of commitment from the organization—a commitment that's the first step toward achieving an effective program.

Team planning is essential, but team writing is difficult. Designate a lead writer. Assigning one person as the lead writer is the best way to end up with a smooth-reading proposal that's consistent in tone and voice and that uses terminology uniformly.

Follow directions. If the funder provides instructions, follow them. If you don't understand the instructions, ask for clarification. Failure to follow directions is the leading reason that proposals are not funded.

Make it neat, clean, and easy to read. No typographical errors should mar your final copy. Break up the text: nobody wants to look at a proposal that starts at the top of one page and goes on interminably, without paragraphs or some other breathing space.

If you use a very unusual format, perhaps to attract attention, you risk focusing too much attention on the form of the proposal instead of its content. If you depart from the norm, you had better do it well. One applicant submitted 1,000 proposals in a question-and-answer format, with questions in blue and answers in red, and received not a single response. Recipients probably thought it was a request for a campaign donation.

Avoid jargon. Proposal writing isn't an opportunity to demonstrate your mastery of bureaucratese. Even if the prospective funder seems addicted to jargon, use it only if you really must, and follow it with a clear definition of what you mean. Generalities won't do. For example, the person who is reviewing your "career education" proposal probably has his or her own understanding of what that term means. Tell the funder what you think it means. If a proposal declares teens are "at risk" and says no more, readers may wonder "at risk of what?" and "why?" You need to elaborate. For example, the teens are at risk of dropping out of school because they are frequently absent.

Have an outsider read a draft. To test the clarity of the writing, ask friends or family to read the proposal. Some of your best comments will come from people unfamiliar with your field, not operating with the same assumptions, and unaware of the jargon. Merely passing a proposal around your organization has limitations. Staff may think they know what you mean or may be less than critical because of your role (or theirs). Look for someone who genuinely wants to understand your proposal; who is intelligent but not familiar with your organization or field; and who will give you honest feedback—someone like your grandmother.

Be concise. What is the proper length for a proposal? Just long enough for you to clearly communicate your message, but not long enough to produce a stupor. A ten-page proposal can leave readers hungering for more; a two-page proposal can still put them to sleep.

Be positive. Get yourself up for the task. Remember, you're offering the funder the opportunity to be part of an important, useful undertaking. Writing for grant support is not like writing home from college for money. You don't have to apologize. You're an applicant, not a supplicant. Don't beg!

Don't blow your credibility. Funders build their reputations by supporting winners, not losers, so don't call undue attention to past mistakes. Because few grantmakers want to provide an organization with its last grant on the road to oblivion, avoid statements like this:

> *We are sure that you are aware of the sudden departure of our fiscal officer some three years ago and the subsequent investigations of this agency by the General Accounting Office that resulted in charges against three of our board members.*

If your organization is just emerging from some kind of crisis, acknowledge that. But focus on the recovery—the positive changes taking place. Emphasize the promise and excitement of what's happening now and express confidence that steady forward momentum will continue.

Avoid assumptions. The astute reader finds any number of assumptions or unsupported claims in most grant proposals. Here are a few examples.

- The proposal includes almost no information about the applicant organization because the writer assumes the funder knows all about it.

- The proposal describes the national scope of the problem but fails to document its existence in the community to be served.

- The proposal presumes a cause-and-effect relationship but doesn't back it up. For example, children from poor families are said to be at increased risk for failure in school, but no evidence is presented to show the relationship between poverty and school failure.

- The proposal declares that a program is unique but fails to show why.

Statements starting with "we believe" signal an assumption. Without solid evidence behind a statement, it won't carry much weight. Replacing beliefs with evidence is a check on logic, results in a more coherent proposal, and shows the funder you know what you're talking about. If you can't support a statement, consider eliminating it.

Present enough evidence to support your position, and no more. Don't overkill. Pages of tables, charts, and graphs will probably not be read and too often fail to make the point. Cite sources of data in the body of the proposal and avoid footnotes. A proposal's not a doctoral dissertation.

Choose words wisely. Language is powerful and its use in a proposal must be sensitive and respectful. Careless word selection can taint the proposal with hints of sexism, racism, or countless other "isms" even though none is meant. Are teens in the after-school program "young women" or "girls"? What terminology should you use for men returning to the community from jail?

Make it human. Quotes and stories express the feelings and experiences of the people your organization serves. They engage readers in a way that statistics and other hard data can't. The story of how a problem affects a particular family makes hard data human. Include voices of real people telling how a problem or solution touches their lives.

Balance. This is an important concept in proposal writing. For example, during one week The Grantsmanship Center received an order for 2,000 reprints of its original *Program Planning & Proposal Writing* publication from the U.S. Department of Labor and another order for one reprint from a proposal writer who said:

> *"I'm from a small town in New Hampshire working for the mayor. Last week City Hall burned to the ground and, what's worse, my only copy of PP&PW went with it. Please send another copy immediately. I can't manage without it."*

The quote from the New Hampshire proposal writer has human interest, and the statistic of the 2,000-copy order from a large government agency shows respect for the publication and adds credibility on a grander scale.

Balance can mean balancing statistics and quotes. It can also mean including the opinions of clients along with those of noted experts. When you're attuned to the concept of balance, your proposal will be better documented and more enjoyable to read.

PROPOSAL PLANNING

- Include others
- Examine the problem
- Determine what change is possible
- Select methods for optimal results

PROPOSAL BASICS

- Follow funder guidelines
- Make it easy & pleasant to read
- Avoid jargon
- Have an outsider read it
- Be concise
- Get "up" for the work
- Focus on the positive
- Avoid assumptions
- Choose words wisely
- Make it human
- Balance the content

Private vs. Government Grantmakers

The importance of planning and the basic principles already covered apply to all grant proposals. That said, there are differences in working with private and corporate foundations and with government agencies. It's crucial to understand these differences. The next two pages offer a quick side-by-side comparison of private and government grantmakers.

PRIVATE AND CORPORATE FOUNDATIONS

Importance of the written proposal varies. The majority of private foundations don't employ staff, and most unstaffed foundations don't accept unsolicited proposals; many contribute only to preselected organizations. With unstaffed foundations, your organization's credibility and personal relationships with foundation trustees and friends are essential. Even when unstaffed foundations do request a written proposal, the quality of the relationship generally trumps the quality of the document.

Staffed private and corporate foundations are also more likely to make grants to organizations with which they have a relationship or have had prior contact. But grantmakers still expect a coherent proposal and the quality of the written proposal carries considerable weight.

Because private funders tend to support organizations they know and trust, relationship building is crucial. Some people are better at building and nurturing contacts than others. The person who develops proposals may not be best for this role. Also consider board members, administrators, and well-connected volunteers.

Proposal requirements. The proposal requirements of private funders range from detailed application guidelines, specific forms, and strict deadlines all the way to no application guidelines and no deadlines at all. When a funder has guidelines, follow them exactly.

Often you'll be asked to submit a letter, and for some funders this will be the only proposal you'll submit. Unless instructed otherwise, keep the letter between three and five pages and structure it according to The Grantsmanship Center Model described in this book. Be sure it addresses all questions asked by the funder and expresses full commitment to the program.

Pre-proposal requirements – LOIs. Sometimes a funder requires an overview of the grant request which is called a *letter of interest*, *a letter of intent*, or a *letter of inquiry*, all using the acronym LOI. LOIs usually serve as a pre-proposal screening device. Based on your LOI, the funder will either request a full proposal or drop you from consideration. But some funders base their award decision on the LOI alone–for them, it's the only proposal you'll submit.

To prepare an LOI, use the same care as with a full proposal. It must be thorough and convey strong commitment to the program. If there are directions, follow them exactly, answering each question the funder asks. If the funder provides no instructions, use the The Grantsmanship Center Model in this book to structure the LOI and keep it to two or three pages. To do this, hammer out your full argument for support, addressing each section of the Model. Then, edit, edit, edit to distill the essence of the request into the LOI.

When a funder's pre-proposal screening device is only a form, if you can, establish personal contact by attaching a cover letter or an email expressing your organization's commitment to the program. See page 182 for more on cover letters.

GOVERNMENT FUNDERS

Quality of the written proposal is critical. Because government grant competitions are meant to be objective, personal or organizational relationships with government staff and elected officials are rarely essential, though they can be useful. With government funders, the proposal carries more weight than the relationship, and a proposal that strictly adheres to the guidelines is imperative.

Most government funders score proposals using a point system. The funder assigns points that can be earned in each section of the proposal and defines the criteria that reviewers will use to allocate those points. If the grant application guidelines don't include the points assigned to each section of the proposal or the scoring criteria, ask for that information. A section worth a lot of points is worth a lot of planning time. That said, it's foolhardy to neglect any section, even those that are assigned fewer points. Work to maximize your total score.

Sometimes, even a wonderful proposal doesn't get funded. If such factors as the geographic distribution of awards or the diversity of target groups are important to the funder, the highest score may not be the deciding factor. Nevertheless, to be in the running, a proposal must receive a high score. Exactly how high depends on the scores of competitors, the funds available, and how far the funds will stretch.

Proposal requirements. Not every private funder has a grant application form or specific proposal guidelines, but government funders have both in ample supply. The concepts included in The Grantsmanship Center Model are consistent with those of most government agencies, but the terms used and the order in which information is requested are often different. Don't substitute our model for the instructions of the funder. If you don't understand the instructions, call or email the funder's designated contact person. Don't guess. Government funders usually disqualify proposals that are incomplete, contain forms that are incorrectly filled out, or fail to follow the instructions exactly.

Pre-proposal requirements. Government funders are less likely than private funders to use pre-proposals as competitive screening devices. But it's not unusual for a government funder to ask for a letter of intent or a notice of intent to apply. This may be a letter of less than a page or even a form to sign and submit. Sometimes this submission is required for entering a funding competition. Usually, its purpose is to let funders know how many proposals to expect so they can begin organizing review panels.

The Grantsmanship Center Model

The Grantsmanship Center Model includes eight sections. Together, they produce a thorough and logical proposal. The first seven sections, Summary through Future Support, are the narrative. The eighth section is the Budget. Each part has a job to do and, because each supports the others, a weakness in one affects the entire proposal.

Failing to sort information into the right section is a common mistake. For example, if the Introduction to the Applicant Organization describes the problem or method rather than the applicant, the entire proposal suffers. Don't let what should be in one section migrate into another.

Focus on concepts, not terminology. The terminology used by funders is inconsistent and even contradictory. What one defines as a "goal," another calls an "objective." What's labeled an "objective" by one may be called a "method" by another. And on it goes. To function successfully in spite of this changeable vocabulary, focus on understanding concepts rather than memorizing terms and definitions.

The Grantsmanship Center Model uses a consistent set of terms, and this book provides a list of other terms commonly used for the same concepts. When you understand the concepts involved in constructing a logical argument for funding, you can translate the variable terms used by funders.

Components of The Grantsmanship Center Model

The first two sections of the proposal, the Summary and Introduction, set the stage for your request for grant support.

Summary. Gives a brief overview of the entire proposal and provides the reader with a context for understanding all other sections, including the Budget. It prepares the reader to review the proposal.

Introduction to the Applicant Organization. Describes the organization that's asking for money. Explains its mission and services, demonstrates credibility, and shows its qualifications for tackling the problem. It's like a résumé for the job.

The next four sections are the core of the argument for grant support. Problem, Outcomes, and Methods are the heart of the argument. Then Evaluation strengthens the package by assuring accountability for implementation and results.

Problem. Describes the situation motivating the applicant to seek a grant. Explains why the situation matters and what's causing it.

Outcomes. Specifies the measurable improvements that the proposed program will produce in the situation described in the Problem Section.

Methods. Responds to the problem's causes. Justifies choice of the approach and presents a detailed plan for program implementation.

Evaluation. Describes how the applicant will assess whether the program activities are proceeding as planned and are producing the expected results.

The last two sections of the proposal, Future Support and Budget, provide critical details concerning the financial aspects of the request.

Future Support. Describes the strategy for sustaining the program or its positive benefits after grant funding ends. Shows why the requested funding is a good investment.

Budget. Delineates expenses to be met by the funder and the resources to be provided by the applicant or others. Shows how expenses are calculated and often provides a written justification for each expense.

The Budget tells the same story as the Methods Section, but in the language of dollars. If implementing the evaluation plan will cost money, the budget will reflect that expense as well.

A Logical Argument for Grant Support

The sections of this model work together to create a compelling case for funding. The Summary and Introduction provide context and credibility. The Problem, Outcomes, and Methods are the heart of the proposal. The Evaluation defines a plan for assessing whether activities are on track and results are being achieved. Future Support provides confidence that plans are in place for sustaining program impact beyond grant funding. The Budget syncs with Methods and Evaluation and shows that costs are appropriate.

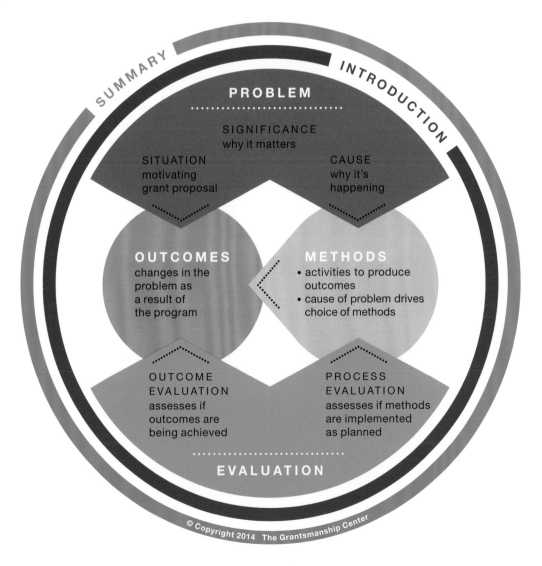

© Copyright 2014 The Grantsmanship Center

Put it before them briefly
so they will read it,
clearly so they will appreciate it,
picturesquely so they will
remember it, and above all,
accurately so they will be
guided by its light.

JOSEPH PULITZER

Summary
The Proposal in a Nutshell

People who review grant proposals want to know up front what a proposal is about and how much money is involved. They don't want to have to plow through the entire document to find out what you're requesting. A concise, clearly written summary is your chance to make a good first impression.

Put it first. Write it last. Don't write the summary until you've completed the proposal. This may seem backward, since the summary will appear at the beginning. But details such as budget figures and sources of outside support often change during the process of writing a proposal. Writing the summary last ensures that it's consistent with all other sections of the document.

Keep it brief. Don't say too much. If the summary begins to look like a mini-proposal, the reviewers may feel no need to read further. Limit the summary to a couple of paragraphs, half of a page at most.

Importance of the Summary

The summary may be all that is read. When applications are screened at the funder's door, funders may use the summary to decide whether a proposal matches their criteria and priorities. It helps them determine whether the proposal is eligible and worth reviewing.

The summary is your first chance to grab the reader's attention. A crisp, interesting summary makes the reader want to learn more.

It orients the reader. It provides context for all other sections. It's difficult to review a proposal when wondering what the point is. A good summary frames the proposal, preparing the reviewer to understand your request.

It tells how much money the applicant is requesting. That way the funder doesn't need to search the Budget Section to figure it out.

It may be widely distributed. Funders sometimes post the summaries of successful proposals on their websites.

Summary
may also be called
· ·
abstract
executive summary
proposal overview
proposal synopsis

Contents of the Summary

Different funders have different requirements. Government agencies usually provide their own forms with specific instructions limiting the number of words or lines of type they'll accept.

Some private funders require applicants to follow an exact format or to complete a cover sheet.

If a funder does not give specific instructions about what to put in the Summary Section, write one to three paragraphs that include:

- Identification of the applicant organization and a sentence or two about its credibility.

- A sentence or two explaining the issue, problem, or need motivating your request.

- A brief statement of the measurable outcomes you expect the program to produce.

- One or two sentences describing the methods you'll use to achieve the outcomes.

- Identification of other organizations that will play major roles, if there are any.

- The time frame for the grant you are seeking. One year? Two? Longer?

- A brief outline of the budget: the amount requested from the funder, the resources others have promised to commit, and the total cost of the program. Make sure the numbers are consistent with the Budget Section later in the proposal.

EXAMPLES: SUMMARY

Here's a not-so-good example.

EXAMPLE 1: Building Responsible Citizens

The long-range goal of this proposed program is to help students develop into adults who think creatively and independently, learn by observation, work together in inquiring teams, develop judgment and decision-making abilities and, most important, adults who can conceive of more satisfactory alternatives to social problems than passive acceptance or militant violence. In short, this program's aim is to help students to grow into adults who actively practice and participate in democratic citizenship.

Not only does this summary leave out just about all of the basics, it's also an exercise in the use of rhetoric. We're not sure what they're really going to do, but it feels like maybe we should salute it.

Here are two examples of good summaries that put it all together. Each is concise but thorough, and sets up the reader nicely for the proposal that will follow:

EXAMPLE 2: Reentry House Program

Reentry House *is a residential program that helps people who have been in jail transition successfully back into the community. Since 1997, when* Reentry House *opened in Kettle, Texas, 80% of the 600 offenders who have participated have stayed out of jail. On average, state and national recidivism rates are much higher, with 50% of offenders committing another crime and returning to jail within a year.*

Reentry House *will open a new residential program in Laurel, Texas, where each year the state prison releases about 50 inmates into the community. This new program will serve 20 offenders per year and expects that approximately 15 of them will stay out of jail.*

Reentry House *has purchased a residence, is completing renovations, and has secured funds for furnishings. The program must now hire and train staff, prepare the residence, and finalize the financial systems that will sustain it. This final stage of start-up will cost $150,000.* Reentry House *will contribute $50,000 of that amount and requests a one-time grant of $100,000 from the Caring Foundation.*

EXAMPLE 3: Arts Alive

Riverside Arts is a nonprofit organization in Cartwright, Utah, that offers a vibrant schedule of performances, exhibitions, and art education programs. Each year, approximately 10,000 people participate in Riverside Arts events and classes. The State Arts Council recognized Riverside Arts' exceptional commitment to the community last June with its annual Art Impact Award.

The National Endowment for the Arts has proven that children who participate in the arts are more likely to excel academically and develop positive skills and behaviors. While 75% of children from moderate- to high-income families in Cartwright are involved in the arts, only 10% of children from low-income families have that advantage. To benefit more low-income children, Riverside Arts will establish Arts Alive. This program will engage and educate 1,500 children from our city's low-income neighborhoods over the course of three years.

The cost of Arts Alive will be $600,000 ($200,000 per year). An amount of $354,000 has already been committed: $225,000 from the State Arts Council, $105,000 from local businesses, and $24,000 in administrative services from Riverside Arts. This proposal requests $82,000 a year for three years—for a total of $246,000.

CHECKLIST: SUMMARY

☐   1. Is at the beginning of the proposal.

☐   2. Identifies the applicant.

☐   3. Includes at least one sentence establishing applicant's credibility.

☐   4. Describes the problem that is compelling the applicant organization
          to submit a grant proposal.

☐   5. Defines the measurable outcomes that the program is expected
          to produce.

☐   6. Provides an overview of the methods to be used.

☐   7. Identifies major partners, if any.

☐   8. Specifies the requested funding period.

☐   9. Includes a budget synopsis stating:

      ☐   a. dollars requested from funder

      ☐   b. cash and in-kind resources contributed by others, if any

      ☐   c. total cost of the program.

☐   10. Is brief—one to three paragraphs, half of a page at most.

☐   11. Is written last.

"Where shall I begin?"
he asked.
"Begin at the beginning,"
the King said,
"and stop when
you get to the end."

LEWIS CARROLL

Alice in Wonderland

Introduction
to the Applicant Organization
Your Organization's Credibility

The Introduction Section tells a funder about the applicant, describing its history, accomplishments, and other evidence of a solid track record. Your assignment is to write an introduction that inspires funder confidence and makes the case that you can deliver what the proposal promises.

Even if you're applying to a funder that is already familiar with your organization, this section still matters. A foundation's board may have new members. A government agency may be using a new review panel. The corporation's managers may have an outdated understanding of your organization's work. A well-written introduction gives funders an up-to-date and accurate view of what your organization does and why they should support it.

If your organization is unknown to a funder, the quality of this section is even more important. Done right, the funder will want to know more about the proposal even if the applicant is a newcomer.

Customize Each Introduction

Most of the information needed to write the Introduction Section can be found within your organization. The website, staff résumés, the annual report, program evaluations, annual service statistics, and letters from supporters and appreciative clients are a few examples of good sources. Once you've gathered the information, establish a system to keep it updated.

The best approach is to draft a comprehensive, all-purpose introduction and then tailor it for each proposal you submit. The Introduction Section of each proposal should highlight your organization's competence and experience as it relates to the specific program for which you are seeking support. And the Introduction Section of each proposal should also be in sync with the particular interests of the funder.

For example, in a request to a local bank for a $5,000 grant to buy groceries for the community food shelf, the introduction should be relatively simple and brief. You'll want to emphasize your organization's role in community affairs and commitment to fighting local hunger. But asking a national foundation for $1 million to fund a new approach in preschool education will require much more. Among other things, you'll need to show that your organization is an innovator, has extensive experience in the field of education, is committed to evaluation, and can handle complex projects and large sums of money.

It's important to keep the Introduction Section tightly focused on your organization. Don't let it stray into a description of the program that you want funded. There will be a place for that later in the proposal.

TWO TYPES OF INFORMATION

The Introduction requires:

- information that describes the organization
- information that establishes its credibility.

Sometimes a single piece of information does double duty by describing the organization and also illustrating its accomplishments. Since you can't include everything in a proposal, choose information for quality, impact, and relevance.

Describe the Organization

Here are some important things a funder will want to know about your organization.

Mission or vision. What drives the organization? Be precise and be brief. Don't dwell interminably on your philosophy, lest you be seen as all thought and no action. Remember, most organizations have a noble sounding mission statement. The funder is interested in how effective the organization actually is in achieving that mission.

History. When and why was the organization founded? Are there major milestones the funder should be aware of? Has it changed in response to community needs? Don't drone on through years of history. Keep it brief and emphasize events that are especially relevant to the program you're proposing.

The board of directors. Board members are legally responsible for your organization's operation, so funders want to know who they are. Quality and diversity are key. Funders

are looking for evidence that your board is composed of experienced volunteers with a good variety of viewpoints and skills. Funders want to see board members' commitment to your organization demonstrated through their contributions of both time and money.

How you handle this in the introduction depends on the page limit of the proposal and the number of board members.

Typically, the Introduction Section describes the board in general terms (i.e., ten members representing business, finance, public safety, education, the faith community, the legal profession, and the people served by the organization). And typically, a full list of the board with a brief biographical sketch of each member is included as an attachment to the proposal.

Size. How big is the organization? How many employees? How many locations? What's the annual budget?

Service area. Describe the area where your organization works. Is it rural, suburban, or urban? How many people live there? Is it predominantly wealthy, middle-class, or poor? Is it safe? What's the ethnic or racial composition? Paint a picture for the reader.

Beneficiaries. Who benefits from the organization's work? Include appropriate demographic information: age, economic status, health, education, or other details to help the reader understand who they are.

Programs. Summarize the organization's major activities. But beware. Just because you know what "case management" is, or what "Project ACT" is, don't assume others will. Include a sentence or two explaining each activity.

Quantity of services. Pin down the numbers. How many and how much?

For example, if an organization rescues stray dogs, what were the service numbers for the last year? How many dogs were rescued? How many nights of shelter were provided? How many dogs were placed in new homes?

Working with others. Although you may not be able to discuss all the collaborative ventures in which your organization participates, highlight a few of the most important and focus on those most closely aligned with the purpose of the grant proposal. Team players accomplish more, and funders expect your organization to work collaboratively with others.

Structure. Funders may request a chart or a synopsis of the organization's structure. If they do, keep it simple. Don't enmesh readers in the intricacies of your organizational structure. They may never find a way out.

Establish Credibility

The funder must have confidence that your organization has the experience and qualifications to deliver what you promise—that the requested grant will be a good investment.

Tailor credibility information to support each proposal. Imagine that your drug abuse treatment organization is seeking a grant to train school staff to recognize the signs of cocaine addiction. You may think it's enough for the Introduction Section of

the proposal to show that your organization has a strong track record of treating cocaine addiction. But it's equally important to show that your organization knows how to conduct a training program, no matter the purpose of the training. The ability to treat doesn't necessarily translate into the ability to train.

Your job is not only to prove your organization's credibility but also to prove it in the specific area the grant program will be addressing.

Don't disparage others. When establishing your organization's credibility, don't do it at the expense of others. Your organization's own experience and results must tell the story.

IDEAS TO STIMULATE YOUR THINKING

Why does your organization stand out? Is it the first of its kind, the only one in the area, the oldest, or the largest? Maybe it has developed a new and imaginative service approach. But don't just say that your organization is unique or uniquely qualified. Prove it with facts.

The Wow! factor. A brief statement describing an extraordinary accomplishment can speak volumes. Here's an example that shows expertise, innovation, and leadership:

> *The Aquarium of Niagara Falls was the first inland aquarium. It was the first aquarium anywhere to use closed-system biological filtration technology and operate entirely with synthetic sea water.*

Quotes. Let other voices make your case. Use supportive quotes from clients, public figures, outside experts, staff at other organizations, newspaper or magazine articles, and even letters, conversations, or speeches. Be sure to get permission when a quote is not from a public source.

Success stories. Testimonials from those you help, and real life stories of success bring abstract information to life, engaging readers in a way that statistics can't. Always be careful to preserve confidentiality.

Special awards. Has your organization been recognized for outstanding service or innovation—something extraordinary, beyond the norm?

Evaluation results. Excerpts from positive program evaluation reports are golden. It's impressive when unbiased experts find that your organization is effective. Documentation is convincing; unsupported claims are not.

Staff expertise. A qualified staff gives funders confidence that the grant will be well managed and the program will be effective. Provide a general description of your team, including such information as years of service, advanced degrees, certifications and licensure, publications, and awards.

Referring agencies. When other agencies refer clients, it's an indication that your organization's work is valued and trusted. Give some examples of referrals received by your organization.

Community support. Donations of time, goods, services, or money from the community indicate high regard for your organization's work.

Finances. Funders must have confidence in your organization's ability to handle money. The gold standard is an annual audit by an independent CPA. Short of that, you can have a CPA certify that your system complies with generally accepted accounting principles or identify the financial management software your organization uses, highlighting that independent cost centers are used for each distinct funding source.

Funding sources. Funding from diverse sources indicates that an organization has a broad base of support. Include a general statement about how your organization is funded and give one or two specific examples of especially impressive supporters.

DESCRIBE THE ORGANIZATION

- Mission or vision
- History
- Board of directors
- Size
- Service area
- Beneficiaries
- Programs
- Quantity of services
- Working with others
- Structure

ESTABLISH CREDIBILITY

- Why your organization stands out
- The Wow! factor
- Quotes
- Success stories
- Special awards
- Evaluation results
- Staff expertise
- Referring agencies
- Community support
- Finances
- Funding sources

IF YOUR ORGANIZATION IS NEW

New organizations face special challenges in demonstrating credibility. But a new organization, like any other, has some kind of history and maybe some early accomplishments to be proud of. Make the most of what you have.

Why the organization was created. Perhaps an urgent community need was the spark. For example, did concerned citizens band together in response to a tragedy? Had the high school dropout rate become alarming?

Community support. Can you document that people in the community supported the formation of the organization? Were there public expressions of support for the new organization's mission?

The founders. Introduce the people behind the founding of the organization and emphasize their credentials. They may be prominent members of the community, experts in their fields, or have a strong record of volunteer service. Some may be passionate about an issue because they have been deeply affected by it.

The board of directors. The qualifications of board members are especially important when an organization has yet to establish a track record. The more impressive they are, the more credible your organization will be.

Services and activities. Often, people provide services or carry out activities before they recognize the need to formalize their work by establishing a nonprofit organization. Describe activities that took place before the organization began operation. What was done that demonstrates the commitment of those who formed the new organization?

Affiliating with others. Having collaborative relationships with well-respected groups in the community is a plus. The new organization can benefit from credibility already established by others.

Raising money. If a new organization has conducted successful fundraisers, that shows it's motivated and organized. If community members have made donations or volunteered, that shows the cause matters to them. If board members personally paid for start-up costs, that shows their dedication. If a foundation, government agency, or business has already provided funding or other types of support, that suggests the new organization is a good investment.

Other Important Points

Your organization's web presence.
Be sure to examine your organization's website and social media as if you were a funder. Most funders check the web presence of applicants. What they find matters. At best, the website and social media trail will enhance your organization's chances of winning a grant. At worst, they will make your organization appear unprofessional, unreliable, or at odds with the grant request. Social networking can inspire or repel. Be sure that whatever carries the organization's name represents it well.

Give the big picture, then zoom in.
When an organization has multiple departments and programs, provide a brief (one- or two-paragraph) description of the entire organization. Then zoom in on the department or program most involved with the proposal and describe it fully. For example, if the state university plans to develop an internship program for art students, the introduction will briefly describe the university, then focus detailed attention on the art department. A brief description of the overall organization provides context to help the reader better understand the part of the organization that will operate the proposed program.

If other organizations are involved. If a significant part of the proposed program will be operated by organizations other than the applicant, provide evidence of each partner's credibility. But provide only a quick summary of the organizations' credentials, not descriptions of their roles in the program (that will come later in the Methods Section). Keep partner introductions brief and be sure the Introduction Section makes it clear that your organization is the applicant.

Don't include groups with minor roles in the Introduction Section. Those will be discussed later in the Methods Section.

WHAT'S IN A NAME?

If an organization's name is misleading or uninformative, it can confuse funders and clients alike. Unfortunately, it can be difficult for people close to the organization to recognize this problem.

For example, The Consumers Network suggests a shopping club rather than a mental health service. The Alliance for Progress could be concerned about almost anything.

Adding a tagline—a short, jazzed-up version of a mission statement—could help. The Alliance for Progress tagline might read "Keeping Our State Green."

In extreme cases, the board may need to consider changing the name to something more descriptive.

This is not an argument for conformity, only a caution that you understand the image that is projected by your organization's name and work with it.

EXAMPLES: INTRODUCTION

EXAMPLE 1: East State Hospital

Since 1960, when East State Hospital was founded, it has received more national and state awards than any other hospital in Iowa. Reporting on its recent Excellence Award from the State Health Department, Jane Evans, editor of the County Newspaper, wrote: "East State Hospital contributes immeasurably to the quality of life in this area. This institution has earned our respect and trust."

East State Hospital is a 250-bed nonprofit medical center located in the city of Bountiful. Its service area includes Tremont County and Jake County. Both counties are suburban and have a combined population of 300,000. East State Hospital has a staff of 2,000, as well as 300 dedicated community volunteers, and serves approximately 68,000 people each year through a full spectrum of in-patient, out-patient, and emergency services. The hospital also maintains a referral relationship with Turring Medical Center, a Level I trauma center located 30 miles away in Middlebury.

East State Hospital's 15-member volunteer board of directors includes professionals from the fields of business, medicine, education, social service, and public service (see attached list), and all members make annual financial contributions. The board is dedicated to the mission of "providing high quality health care to all who need it." The fact that 20% of the people the hospital serves receive charity care is evidence of that dedication. Approximately half of the hospital's revenue comes from Medicaid and Medicare, with the rest coming from commercial insurance, state and local subsidies, patient payments, donations, and fundraising. Annual independent audits consistently document the hospital's exemplary financial management.

In 2013, East State Hospital was awarded Gold status by the National Nurses Organization, which designates hospitals that consistently meet high standards. The thank-you note from May Hernandez is similar to many others the staff receives each year: "I can't thank the staff at East State Hospital enough for the care I got after my surgery. You treated me like a member of your family, and I'm sure that's a big part of why I'm doing well."

> *East State Hospital consistently proves its commitment to quality by exceeding regulatory standards. For example, in 2014, its Infection Control Department initiated state-of-the-art procedures to prevent ventilator-associated pneumonia. As a result, infection rates dropped 30%.*
>
> *Continuing its effort to deliver quality care, the Infection Control Department is now focused on reducing hospital-associated methicillin-resistant Staphylococcus aureus (MRSA) infections. This particularly dangerous type of infection has been steadily increasing at hospitals across the nation, including East State Hospital.*

This provides a good introduction to East State Hospital and establishes its credibility in the area for which it is seeking funding—reducing MRSA infections.

EXAMPLE 2: Self-Esteem Builders

Self-Esteem Builders is a nonprofit delinquency-prevention organization that helps troubled children who are between the ages of seven and 14 years old. The organization's primary approach is mentoring. Adult mentors are matched with troubled children for one year and serve as warm, supportive friends and advocates. Mentors help children identify, face, and deal with personal problems and also help them develop a sense of self-worth.

Self-Esteem Builders responds to troubled children as people rather than problems. We view troubled children as healthy, growing individuals who, though currently troubled, will find their own interests coinciding with the best interests of society if given the right support and a positive environment.

This Introduction is long on philosophy but short on everything else. It fails to answer questions about the organization's experience, competence, and stability.

EXAMPLE 3: Educational Innovation Through Psychometric Assessment

In spite of a decade of educational innovations, little headway has been made in creating a significant alternative to the traditional system of public education—a system which we believe to be ineffectual in an era of rapid social change, one that is groaning under the weight of heavy social burdens while lamenting its own inertia for making integrated efforts toward systematic self-renewal.

That sentence, the first of a seven-page introduction, is typical not only of the introduction, but of the entire proposal. Brevity is a virtue; extensive rhetoric does little more than support the paper industry. "We believe" is inappropriate and unconvincing. Provide sufficient evidence so that the *reader* will believe.

EXAMPLE 4: Jones Rock Affordable Housing Agency—Maintaining a Robust Island Community

"I love this island. My family's history is here and I wanted my children to grow up here, too. But when I had a family of my own, we couldn't afford a home and thought we'd have to leave. With help from the island's Affordable Housing Agency we now have a home on the island. I'm thankful every day that we're still here."

— Tim Gunderson, Fisherman

The island of Jones Rock is located four miles off the coast of Northern Washington State and covers twenty square miles. While 850 people live on the island year-round, the population swells to 1,350 in the summer when second-home owners arrive. Most year-round residents come from families who have lived here for many generations and make a modest living from the sea. The high demand for housing, created by the steadily increasing number of summer residents, has caused prices to rise. Many young island families now find it difficult to afford a place to live.

In 1997, concerns that younger generations were being priced off the island prompted the City Council to study the situation. After examining issues ranging from health care and housing to fuel costs and education, the study identified the high cost of housing as the most serious problem. In 1998, the Jones Rock Affordable Housing Agency (the Agency) was established to address that challenge.

The Agency's mission is to make Jones Rock housing affordable for year-round residents with low and moderate incomes. The Board of Directors includes three City Council members, two low- to moderate-income residents, two vacation homeowners, and three additional community members (see attached list). The executive director, Rupert Belten, is a native islander. He completed advanced degrees in community development and led an affordable housing agency on the mainland for ten years before returning to Jones Rock. With a staff of three and an annual operating budget of $200,000 (excluding housing development costs), the Agency is recognized as a model of "efficiency, effectiveness, and community involvement." (See attached commendation from the State Housing Authority.)

After an assessment of island housing, the Agency established a three-phase, 15-year plan to build 20 low- to moderate-income homes and ten affordable apartments by 2017. Phases one and two are complete and include 15 homes and five apartments that now house 75 islanders. Four banks, three foundations, and the State Housing Authority have provided funding. In the last eight years, year-round and summer residents have donated over $650,000.

The Agency has completed phases one and two on time and within budget despite rapid changes in the cost of construction. Annual audits by an independent CPA have consistently shown excellent financial management (latest audit attached). The Agency is now ready to complete phase three of its initial plan, which will provide up to 16 islanders with shelter.

Speaking before the City Council in October, Sarah Rosen, chairperson of the board, voiced the philosophy and commitment of the Jones Rock Affordable Housing Agency: "We're committed to a diverse island community that embraces all of us who care about this special place."

This is an interesting and well-developed introduction that hits all the necessary points.

CHECKLIST: INTRODUCTION TO THE APPLICANT ORGANIZATION

☐   1. Clearly establishes who is applying for funding.

☐   2. Describes the organization and its work:

    ☐   a. mission or vision

    ☐   b. history

    ☐   c. beneficiaries

    ☐   d. service area

    ☐   e. programs and services

    ☐   f. quantity of services

    ☐   g. networking and collaboration

    ☐   h. size of organization (budget, number of staff, etc.)

    ☐   i. board of directors

    ☐   j. organizational structure, if this adds clarity or is requested.

☐   3. Establishes the organization's credibility.

    ☐   a. Demonstrates the organization's expertise in the program area for which it is seeking funds.

    ☐   b. Provides evidence of past accomplishments.

☐   4. Uses hard data (statistics and other objective evidence).

☐   5. Uses soft data (anecdotes, quotes, and stories).

☐   6. Briefly introduces partner organizations that have major roles.

☐   7. Does not stray into a description of the proposed program.

☐   8. Leads logically to discussion of the problem.

"Then you should say
what you mean,"
the March Hare went on.

"I do," Alice hastily replied;
"at least—at least I mean what I say—
that's the same thing, you know."

"Not the same thing a bit!" said the Hatter.

"Why, you might just as well say that
'I see what I eat' is the same thing as
'I eat what I see!'"

LEWIS CARROLL

Alice in Wonderland

Problem
The Reason for Your Proposal

This is the most critical part of your proposal because it explains why your organization is seeking a grant.

Your organization may be targeting a health-related problem, such as the high rate of HIV infection in the city, or taking on an environmental issue, like the pollution of a lake. Perhaps the high school band can't afford travel to a national competition, or the state history museum has an opportunity to bring a rare exhibit to the area. Whether you define these as problems, needs, or opportunities, any of them could be the motivation for a funding proposal. Here, we call it the "problem."

Problem may also be called

need
needs assessment
problem analysis
problem discussion
problem justification
problem statement
situational analysis

Until you can understand and define the problem you're concerned about, you can't plan a program to address the situation effectively, and you can't write a logical and convincing grant proposal.

Defining the problem sets your proposal train on its track. If you want to get to Chicago, it would be most distressing to end up in Seattle. Asking and answering three primary questions will keep the problem discussion on track.

Three Primary Questions

1. **What is the situation motivating your organization to take action?**
   Concisely state the concern. Has the rate of HIV infection in the city increased? Have recent tests shown that the nearby lake has become polluted?

   Who or what is affected? If extinction of the eastern box turtle is the concern, tell the reader about that species and its role in the ecosystem. If HIV infection is the concern, paint a picture of the people affected, including relevant characteristics such as the age, gender, income level, ethnicity, educational level, health status, or other data appropriate to the situation.

   How are they affected? It's not enough to report that a certain segment of the population has a high rate of HIV infection. Explain how that diagnosis changes their lives. What are the short- and long-term health implications? Does it affect employment, finances, and families? It's not enough to prove that a lake is polluted and to identify the species of animals and the towns that are affected. Explain how they are affected. Are fish dying? Is it changing the economy? For example, are marina owners, going out of business?

   What's the magnitude? Quantify the problem. Show how many people are affected. Let the reader know if the rate of HIV infection in the community is higher than in others or is increasing more rapidly—and by how much. Even if it's not, offer some evidence of the magnitude of the situation.

2. **What is the significance?**
   Tell the reader why the situation matters. Why this and why now? What will happen if no one takes action? Help the funder understand the urgency.

3. **What are the causes?**
   Document the causes of the situation. When documentation is not available, investigate. Don't make assumptions. Only when an organization understands the causes of the problem can it begin to suggest solutions.

Five Guiding Principles

1. Be sure the applicant's mission and the problem align.

The problem your organization plans to address must be in harmony with its stated mission. Take, for example, a drug treatment center that wants to address the problem of homelessness among its clients. Because the center's mission is drug treatment and recovery, its proposal must make the connection between homelessness and addiction. If the proposal discusses homelessness in isolation, it has failed to achieve mission alignment.

2. Focus on the beneficiaries, not the applicant organization.

An organization is valuable only because of what it provides to its beneficiaries. An organization's budget crisis is not, in and of itself, the basis for a proposal. A funder would ask, "So what? In what way will the beneficiaries be affected if programs are shut down?"

3. Document the problem in your community.

If the problem your organization is addressing is of statewide, national, or international scope, give a quick summary of the problem's broad reach to anchor the local situation in a larger context. But keep that overview brief.

Focus on the local problem. You must present evidence that it exists in your community and that it is significant there.

Use comparative statistics if you can get them, but only when they support the argument. The proposal's job is not to prove that your community has the worst problem. Its job is to document that the problem exists in your community and that it is significant. A community may have a substantial problem even if data indicate the local situation is less severe than state or national averages.

Be prepared to conduct a thorough research effort—everything from an online investigation and a bibliography search to digging through statistics at city hall and surveying community opinion. Using a variety of evidence from data sources like those shown below helps make proposals both persuasive and interesting.

- *First-hand testimony.* The most moving and convincing quotes and stories are likely to come from those immediately affected by the situation.

- *Perspectives of knowledgeable people.* Experts, community members, and your organization's own staff may be able to provide helpful insight.

- *Data and more data.* Collecting statistics, reports, and other data to support your proposal is vital. Look for data within your own organization and ask other community groups. Examine the minutes of meetings at which the problem was discussed. Track down pertinent reports and studies issued by government agencies, academic experts, and other authoritative sources. Scan the media, including reputable Internet sites, for quotes and facts that can add impact.

When presenting a great deal of data, you can use charts, graphs, and other visual tools to deliver information succinctly and give the reader a break from a wall of text. But don't overdo it. Saturating the proposal with charts and graphs will numb the reader. If you do include graphics, also include explanations so they won't be misinterpreted.

Be selective. The quality and freshness of data affect a proposal's credibility, so use information that's authoritative and as current as possible. A quote on the Internet from someone with strong opinions about pollution but no credentials is not authoritative. A quote from the website of the state's Natural Resources Department is. You may want to use data from an older study because it is authoritative and there has been nothing to replace it. If so, briefly explain your decision.

4. **Involve people who are affected.**
Get the perspective of those directly impacted. They can help you understand the situation, its significance, and its causes in ways that no one else can. They'll help you avoid wrong assumptions so you can design a program that genuinely responds to their needs. A proposal that includes the voices and views of those affected is more valid and will have more impact.

5. **Match the organization's capacity.**
Sometimes a problem is just too big and an organization can't tackle the whole thing. In that case, give a quick overview of the entire problem, then explain what part your organization will take on. For example, a shelter that doesn't have the capacity to assist all homeless families in the city might limit its new program to families with children. The problem discussion must then detail the difficulties of homeless families in the community who have children.

Hard Data & Soft Data

The most convincing proposals contain a mix of hard and soft data, carefully chosen for maximum impact.

Hard data are quantifiable. Examples include statistics, research studies, and graphs that prove the existence and magnitude of a problem. When hard data are accurate and relevant, they lend validity to the proposal. They also indicate that you have rigorously examined the issue.

Soft data reflect people's feelings and experiences. They add context and real life images to a proposal that can't be matched by statistics.

Balance statistics and research with quotes and anecdotes. Include views from experts—both professionals and those affected by the situation. A proposal with both hard and soft data is better documented and more enjoyable to read.

Know your funder. You may have to adjust the balance between hard and soft data to satisfy the preferences of a specific funder. Some, like the National Institutes of Health, expect a level of hard data that's well above the usual requirements of a foundation, while others want numbers but are more interested in quotes and anecdotes.

Here are two examples of the presentation of hard data. Which do you find more compelling?

EXAMPLES: Hard Data

1. *In May 2014 the State Environmental Protection Agency reported 0.95 parts per million of mercury in the fish of Dolphin Bay. The U.S. Center for Disease (report number 2A75, 2014) warned that fish contaminated at levels above 0.3 are not safe to consume and that those who ingest contaminated fish are at significantly elevated risk for a variety of serious health concerns. Observations by Marine Patrol (Boat 77, July 2014 report) indicate that the bay continues to function as a primary recreational area with fishing the most popular of pursuits. A recent one-day community survey documented that 80% of the 120 fishermen responding consider the posted warnings to be excessive. They continue to consume these fish because of economic disadvantages or because they do not consider mercury contamination a serious threat to their future health, or both.*

2. *Dolphin Bay's fish are dangerously contaminated with mercury. According to the State Environmental Protection Agency's June 2014 report, these fish contain an average mercury level of 0.95 per million. This rate is 32% above the level documented as a health hazard. Eating mercury-contaminated fish has been directly linked to cancer, impaired immunity, liver damage, and reproductive problems. Further, children of mothers who eat mercury-contaminated fish while pregnant are more likely to have developmental delays. This sobering data is based on the U.S. Center for Disease report dated June 2014. On July 5, 2014, the Healthy Bay Society conducted a survey: 96 of the 120 fisherman responding on that typical weekday said that they would be eating their catch because they didn't believe the posted warnings or because they relied on the fish as a staple of their diet, or both.*

Although both examples provide worthwhile data, the language in example 1 is flat. The vague phrase "serious health concerns" doesn't have the same impact as the list in example 2 of cancer, liver damage, and children harmed by chemicals. Example 1 requires the reader to calculate the difference between 0.95 and 0.3 to understand the level of danger. Example 2 does the math, telling the reader that pollution levels are 32% higher than acceptable. Make data accessible and humanize its presentation when possible, as in the "children of mothers who eat mercury contaminated fish while pregnant."

Which of the following examples for soft data do you think is more effective?

EXAMPLES: Soft Data

1. *"The fact that mercury contamination of the bay's fish exceeds safe levels is a serious issue. The warning signs posted at Dolphin Bay are explicit and reference the state report, yet many people continue to fish there and to consume what they catch. It is my understanding that some of them don't believe the warnings, and that many must get their food from those polluted waters because they don't have other options. Additional deterrents must be enacted. As a healthcare practitioner I know that the situation is grave."*

   — Julio Kindler, M.D., Local Physician

2. *"That little bit of chemicals won't hurt us," said the fisherman, turning away from a sign that warned Do Not Eat Fish From This Bay! Even though the sign clearly listed serious health problems caused by eating mercury-contaminated fish, the fisherman, a day laborer with three children and a pregnant wife, believed the bay's fish were safe to eat. He and a crowd of more than a hundred others were fishing in Dolphin Bay on July 5, 2014. "I fish here about twice a week." he said. "Eating from the bay is how we get by. It's how I feed my family."*

Both quotes have value. Dr. Kindler's quote is an authoritative statement of concern. But he's not eating the fish; he's not personally in danger. The story of the fisherman is personal and is almost guaranteed to engage those who read it.

Caution! Lack of the Method Is Not the Problem

Declaring that the problem is the lack of your proposed method is a common and dangerous mistake. It devastates the logic of a proposal and sets up an argument that chases its tail.

If, for example, an applicant claims, "The problem is that there is no teen center in this community," then the logical outcome would be that the community will have a teen center. The logical method would be to open a teen center, and the evaluation would assess if a teen center exists.

This is not a convincing and logical argument for funding. A funder's first reaction to it will likely be, "So what? Why should I care?" Nowhere in this discussion are teens mentioned. We don't even know if there are teens in the community and, if there are,

what problems or challenges they face. In this argument, the teen center—the method—is a solution in search of a problem.

Often an organization gets so caught up in its proposed program, its approach, its methodology, that it fails to logically think through the problem it's trying to solve. Creating the program becomes all important—the means inadvertently become the end.

To avoid this mistake, questions need to be asked. What is the problem the community is concerned about? Who or what is affected, and how? What is the magnitude and severity of the situation? Why should we care? Why is this happening? What's the cause of the situation?

First the applicant must examine the situation: gather data; talk to teens, parents, police, and others in the community; conduct a survey; participate in community meetings.

After a thorough exploration, a rough sketch of the problem might look like this:

Situation causing concern: Over the past two years, the community has experienced a well-documented increase in vandalism that police attribute to teens. After school, large numbers of teens congregate in unsupervised locations. Few teens participate in community activities and events. Teens say they're not valued by the community.

PROBLEM
There's no teen center

OUTCOME
We'll have a teen center

METHOD
Find space, hire staff, offer programming

EVALUATION
Easy: Is there a teen center?

BUT WAIT!
Where are the teens? What's the real problem?

Significance. Vandalism harms the community, and teens who vandalize property are at risk of escalating antisocial behavior that can result in long-term problems. Parents consider the unsupervised gatherings unsafe and police report that the gatherings contribute to negative behavior. Because few teens participate in community activities, the community is losing the benefit of positive teen energy and is failing to develop future civic leaders.

ROUGH SKETCH OF CORE ARGUMENT FOR FUNDING

PROBLEM

Situation: Teen vandalism; unsupervised teen gatherings; alienated teens

Significance: Teens unsafe & antisocial behavior places them at risk of long-term problems. Community harmed by vandalism, losing positive teen input, not developing future civic leaders.

Cause: Inadequate positive teen activities; Inadequate opportunities to engage with and contribute to community

METHODS

Establish teen center; Engage teens in planning space, programs, policies; Provide best practice teen activities; Offer teen leadership institute; Engage teens in community service; Engage adult volunteers.

OUTCOMES

- Decreased teen vandalism
- Decreased unsupervised teen gatherings
- Increased teen participation in positive activities
- Increased teen engagement in community
- Teens feel more valued by community

EVALUATION

Process: Teen center opened on schedule? Operating as planned? Engaging # teens expected? How are teens engaged? What do teens think?

Outcome: To what degree are vandalism and unsupervised gatherings decreasing? To what degree is teen participation in positive activities and in the community increasing? Do teens feel more valued?

Causes. Many teens report that they are bored and that they do not feel valued by the community. The applicant's research shows that sports are the only organized after-school activity available for teens, but 60% don't play sports. The applicant also found that teens are not welcome to hang out in local cafes; have extremely limited access to positive, interesting activities; have few comfortable, supervised places to socialize; and have limited opportunities to contribute to the community.

With this sketch of the problem, a logical argument for grant support begins to fall into place. The applicant will propose outcomes related to teens' decreased negative activity, increased positive engagement, and increased sense of being valued. The method for achieving the desired outcomes will be a teen center program that provides interesting activities; offers a comfortable, supervised space for teens to socialize; and encourages teen leadership and meaningful community engagement. The program evaluation will assess whether the teen center program is being implemented as planned and is producing the desired changes in the problem.

Caution! The Cause of the Problem Is Not the Problem Itself

Suppose a new technology has been shown to improve cancer treatment, but the local hospital doesn't have it. The hospital might argue that its lack of the technology is the problem.

But wait: how are patients affected? If the closest treatment center using the technology requires a four-hour drive three times a week, it could be beyond the reach of anyone without a car or unable to tolerate the travel. Or waiting lists may be so long that delayed treatment results in slower rates of remission or recovery.

The hardship or harm experienced by the patients is the problem. The fact that the hospital doesn't have the technology is important only if it affects the patients.

Although the hospital's lack of the technology may be the *cause* of the problem, the lack of technology is not, in and of itself, the problem.

EXAMPLES: PROBLEM

Every element of a grant proposal is an opportunity to build credibility or to lose it. Here are three examples of proposal writing in which the authors try to explain the situation that is compelling their organization to seek a grant. Which one is on the right track?

EXAMPLE 1: The Playground at Hancock Park Is Unsafe

The playground equipment at Hancock Park is 40 years old and has been in poor condition for the last ten years. The slides, swings, and seesaws are rusty and broken and the area has become a hangout for vandals who further damage the equipment. Because the playground is so unattractive and unsafe, many parents will not take their children there.

In the last year, eight children were injured when they were pinched by rusty metal or fell because guard rails had been pulled off. It is time to replace the playground equipment to make the park attractive and safe.

Unfortunately, repairing the playground is not a priority for the town council. Because a parents' group built the playground, council members say parents should solve the problem. Our parents' group must find funding to improve the equipment within six months or the council will turn the playground into a parking lot. The council has agreed to serve as the fiscal agent for this grant application to give us a chance to raise the necessary money.

The parents and children involved have suffered with this situation for years and are determined to reclaim the playground somehow. Because this is the only playground in town, we all agree that it should not be closed and we are confident we can agree on the best way to fix it. The bottom line is that the situation is dangerous and something must be done to improve it.

What's a funder to do? The situation cries out for intervention, yet the applicant does not inspire confidence. Where have these people been for the last ten years? Why are they letting their children use dangerous equipment? Why does the city keep the playground open if it's in such dismal repair? The city has little commitment to the project, and the parents appear disorganized. After reading this, a parking lot doesn't seem like such a bad idea.

This is what could be called a self-indicting argument. The flaws in this proposal may seem obvious to many readers. But proposal writers can lose perspective and become oblivious to the funder's point of view when their organizations are in dire straits. Funders are not interested in sinking money into a desperate organization that doesn't have a plan and doesn't appear to have capable leadership.

EXAMPLE 2: Malone Arts Center Facing Drastic Budget Cuts

The City of Malone has economic problems. The tax base has crumbled because our manufacturing and textile jobs have moved overseas. Some corporations have torn down their vacant factories to avoid paying taxes. The remaining small businesses find it hard to survive.

The city budget is being cut this year, municipal services are being reduced, and city support for many nonprofit organizations is being slashed or eliminated.

The Malone Arts Center brings life into our city—3,700 people come to our programs every year. Even though our board of directors made a presentation to the city council, our budget cut was still drastic. In July, our annual funding allocation will be reduced from $50,000 to $20,000.

While people are struggling to meet basic needs, there's little money to spare. Admission to our gallery is free, and the small fee we charge for art classes covers only materials and instructor stipends. Businesses donate food for openings and contribute office supplies, but they can't do more. Our two annual fundraising events don't bring in enough to support our summer art camp or our staff.

Without additional funding, the center will be forced to lay off staff and make extensive program cuts.

The applicant is concerned because it will soon lose staff and programs, but why should we care? The center has not made a strong case that cutting its budget will hurt residents of the city. Will senior citizens lose the creative and social benefits of art classes? If the summer art camp closes its doors, will children be left home alone while parents work? Will artists lose their exhibit space? Maybe.

This discussion misses the mark because it focuses on the organization rather than the people it intends to help. An organization is valuable only because of what it provides to its beneficiaries. A funding cut to an organization is not, in and of itself, a problem. A funder would ask, "So what? How will the community be affected?"

EXAMPLE 3: Elders With Untreated Depression Are in Danger

Of the 5,250 people in Hill County who are over age 70, approximately 600 suffer from clinical depression, but only about half are being treated. Without proper treatment, depressed elders are much more likely to lose their independence or die from preventable causes.

Caring for Our Own, a statewide county-by-county study, was released by the State Health Department last year. It showed that only about half of the elders in Hill County who experience depression receive treatment. It also identified three primary reasons for this:

> *1. Symptoms, such as fatigue and forgetfulness, are often attributed to other physical conditions or dementia.*

> *2. Physicians do not routinely screen elders for depression.*

> *3. Elders often reject treatment because they don't believe it will help or are afraid of the cost.*

Whether a physician fails to properly diagnose depression or an elder refuses treatment, the results can be equally disastrous. Depression and Elders, a 2014 National Research Council study, reported that people over age 70 with untreated depression are 80% more likely to enter a nursing home or die of preventable causes than peers who are not depressed or who receive treatment.

Discussions with Hill County service providers and residents tell the story behind the facts and figures.

Robert Gutierrez, Executive Director of the Council on Aging, says that about half of the elders referred last year suffered from self-neglect caused by depression, rather than dementia or physical disability. Many of the depressed elders were not eating, bathing, or taking their medications, and were living in unsanitary conditions.

Ruth Wolsky, M.D., a geriatric psychiatrist with Hill County Mental Health Clinic, says she sees the problem much too frequently. "People expect dementia, and because of that, both family members and physicians miss the depression; they often get it wrong."

"It's common for elders who arrive for placement in skilled nursing facilities to suffer from untreated depression," said Jasmine Curry, director of Cedar Lane Nursing Home. "Once they're diagnosed, we can treat the depression. But if there's already too much physical and mental damage, they'll never go home."

These local experts agreed that, even when elders are suffering, they are reluctant to seek treatment for depression. One elder interviewed by clinic staff voiced the prevailing attitude, "Why should I spend my money when the doctor won't help anyway?"

It's not just elders who suffer when depression goes untreated. Shelly Brighton, the daughter of a local elder, was anxious to share her story, hoping it would help others:

> *"I live out of the area so I could only visit Dad every couple of months. Mom died last year and so it seemed understandable that Dad had the 'blues.' Last month, when I got there, he hadn't been eating or washing and was so ill that he had to be hospitalized, then moved to a nursing home. He was clinically depressed and I never knew it. After treatment, he seemed more like himself, but he'd already deteriorated so much that he couldn't live on his own any more. I was supposed to look after him and I failed."*

In addition to the pain of elders and their families, untreated depression takes a financial toll on the community. The expense of treating a depressed elderly person on an out-patient basis averages $3,000 per year (U.S. Mental Health Statistics Board, 2013). In contrast, a five-day stay in a hospital costs about $13,000 (Hospital Cost Board, 2014). A year in a nursing home averages $65,000 (Nursing Home Costs Council, 2014).

The Hill County Mental Health Clinic Board of Directors voted unanimously at its July meeting to address this critical problem. The County Physicians Association has enthusiastically agreed to collaborate with us. (See attached letter of commitment.) Together, our organizations will increase diagnosis and treatment of depressed elders and decrease hospitalizations and preventable deaths.

The Hill County Mental Health Clinic is on the right track. This is an interesting and logical discussion of a problem that is affecting the community. It's easy to read and free of jargon. It defines the situation that concerns the applicant organization, and it mixes statistics with quotes from authorities and those affected. The partnership with the County Physicians Association supports the credibility of the applicant. All in all, a good job.

CHECKLIST: PROBLEM

☐   1. Documents the problem:

    ☐   a. who or what is affected

    ☐   b. how they are affected

    ☐   c. the magnitude and severity of the situation.

☐   2. Explains the problem's significance.

☐   3. Clearly identifies and documents the causes of the problem.

☐   4. Aligns with the applicant organization's mission.

☐   5. Focuses on problems of beneficiaries, not the applicant organization.

☐   6. Documents the problem in the applicant's community.

☐   7. Is supported by a mix of data:

    ☐   a. hard data—facts, statistics, research

    ☐   b. soft data—quotes, stories.

☐   8. Incorporates input from those affected by the problem.

☐   9. Scope does not exceed applicant organization's capacity.

☐   10. Does not define the problem as the lack of the proposed method.

☐   11. Does not identify the cause of the problem as the problem itself.

☐   12. Does not tarnish credibility of applicant organization—is not self-indicting.

☐   13. Provides a smooth transition to outcomes.

In every enterprise
consider where
you would come out.

PUBLILIUS SYRUS

Outcomes
Expected Results of the Program

Grantmakers want to know what benefits a program will produce during the period of grant funding. The benefits—we call them outcomes—that you define in this section will be the criteria you'll use to judge the program's effectiveness.

The connection between the problem and the expected outcomes must be direct. For example, if the problem is that children have poor reading skills, then the outcome will be better reading skills. If the problem is that a high percentage of those who return to the community from prison go back to prison, then the outcome will be a decrease in recidivism.

Outcomes may also be called

· ·

results

objectives

program impact

program objectives

outcome objectives

performance objectives

behavioral objectives

program aims

goals

Use concise statements to define the specific and measurable results the program is expected to produce. Although program outcomes are expectations—targets that can rarely be guaranteed—write them in positive and declarative language. Don't equivocate or hedge with statements such as "we hope that" or "we believe." Stating outcomes with conviction conveys confidence that your program will produce results.

Don't Confuse Outcomes With Methods

Mixing up methods and outcomes is one of the most common mistakes in proposal writing and it is often fatal. It's critical to distinguish between them.

The difference between methods and outcomes is the difference between means and ends. The means are the activities—the methods (which we discuss in the next chapter). The ends are the results—the outcomes.

If you begin your outcome statements with words like these, you are sure to be talking about methods and not outcomes.

- **To provide**
- **To offer**
- **To create**
- **To distribute**
- **To implement**
- **To develop**

If you use words like these, you're more likely to be describing outcomes:

- **To increase**
- **To reduce**
- **To decrease**

But take care. Using words like increase, decrease, and reduce does not guarantee that you've described an outcome. For example, "to increase the number of children who receive tutoring from ten to 20" is not an outcome. Why? Because this phrase describes the actions of the applicant organization, rather than the results of the tutoring. The tutoring is part of the method. It's not an outcome.

Methods are what your organization will do to produce a change in the problem. The hours of service the organization will provide and the numbers of people it will serve are aspects of the method. Purchasing equipment, distributing brochures, and presenting classes are all methods as well.

Outcomes describe the results created by the methods. Improved air quality, decreased traffic congestion, and quicker response time by the fire department are examples of outcomes.

THESE ARE OUTCOMES

Of the 70 fifth graders who read at third-grade level, 21 (30% of the target group) will increase their reading skills by two grade levels within six months, as measured by the state standard achievement test for reading.

Between June 2015 and December 2015 hospital data will show that no more than 60 patients suffer secondary infections, a 50% decrease from the current six-month average of 120.

By the end of the school year, 56% of the 80 students who smoke 10 or more cigarettes a day will have changed their smoking habits: 20 students (25%) will report they have quit smoking, and another 25 students (31%) will report smoking fewer cigarettes each day.

THESE ARE METHODS

To provide 70 fifth graders with six months of intensive tutoring and reading-skill development.

To implement a new hospital-wide hand-washing procedure.

To create an aggressive peer education program involving at least 30 anti-smoking youth activists.

Answer Five Questions

Program outcomes are concise statements that define the following:

1. **Who or what will change?**
   The people or things that will change as a result of the program must align with those described in the Problem Section.

2. **How many?**
   Give the number of people or things that will change.

3. **How much change will take place?**
   Use numbers to tell the reader the exact amount of change that's predicted, and be sure to identify the starting point for measurement. Proposing a 20% decrease in the response time of an ambulance service doesn't mean anything until it's compared to the current response time. A "20% decrease in response time, from ten to eight minutes," is a concrete statement of what the program intends to accomplish.

4. **What type of change?**
   The type of change will depend on the problem described. If the problem is obesity, a decrease in the body mass index of participants may be the desired improvement. If the problem is the near-extinction of the Bactrian camel, an increase in the number of that species or perhaps an improvement in its habitat might be proposed.

Generally, program outcomes propose decreases in negative behaviors or conditions or increases in skills, behaviors, or conditions that are positive.

5. **When?**
   Over what time period will the proposed outcomes take place? Establishing a realistic time frame for accomplishing outcomes helps staff set logical points for measuring and reporting progress.

In addition to answering the five questions above, outcomes often briefly note how the expected change will be documented. This is done so that the reviewer won't have to thumb through the Evaluation Section to figure it out. This isn't required but can be helpful.

SMART Outcomes

The acronym SMART is a useful tool to help proposal writers develop better outcomes. Outcomes should be **S**pecific, **M**easurable, **A**chievable, **R**easonable, and **T**ime-Limited— SMART. We'd love to give someone credit for this handy tool, but even though it's widely used, it's not clear where it originated.

Here are two SMART outcome statements.

Thirty of the 40 elderly patients (75%) referred to the clinic for depression will enter treatment within two weeks of referral.

Within two months of entering treatment, medical reports will document that, 25 of the 30 elderly patients (83%) are: (1) stabilized; (2) following doctor's orders; and (3) no longer classified as severely depressed.

Unfortunately, many grant proposals include outcomes that are vague rather than specific and measureable. Here are a couple of examples. The following is for a program to address the problem of hunger in a low-income neighborhood.

The program will improve the opportunity for low-income people to gain access to federal food and nutrition programs by employing an outreach worker.

How would "improved opportunity" be measured, and why would anyone care? The problem is hunger. This outcome stops short of proposing a meaningful, specific, and measurable change in the problem. Employing an outreach worker is a method, not an outcome.

How compelling is the next outcome for a program that will address the problem of family homelessness?

The Getting-Home Program will help homeless families achieve a high quality of life and build a future filled with hope.

Well, it's a nice thought, but it's not a program outcome. How many homeless families will benefit? In what way? To what degree? Over what period of time? If the problem is that families are homeless, the outcome should specify how the applicant organization expects to change that problem.

How Much Change?

Predicting how much change will take place can be tricky because you don't want to promise more than can be delivered or to underestimate what can be accomplished.

Before committing, think hard about your organization's experience in this field, especially any previous work that involved a similar target population or similar programs. Look at the results achieved by other organizations when operating similar programs. Get expert advice. For example, if your project is designed to improve reading skills, consult a remedial-reading specialist.

How do the scope and intensity of the services stack up against the severity of the problem? For example, a drug-treatment group that meets once a week for one hour can't be expected to produce the same results as a program that includes weekday one-hour sessions and weekend activities.

In rare cases, when it's not possible to estimate the degree of change that the program will produce, you may have to propose a "statistically significant" change— one that could not have occurred by chance. Use this approach only when there is no other option and be sure that someone skilled in statistics helps with designing and implementing the program evaluation.

Even if you've carefully estimated the benefits a program will produce, those benefits could seem overly optimistic or unambitious. If you think this could happen, include a brief justification of why your organization thinks the degree of change proposed is realistic.

Outcomes vs. Goals

Outcomes define benefits expected during the finite period of grant funding. Those benefits will often contribute to a larger long-term change. That long-term change is sometimes called a "goal." And in the variable terminology of the grants world, what some call goals, others call "long-term outcomes" or "program impact." Goals, long-term outcomes, and program impact tend to be expressed in broad and lofty language.

In contrast, outcomes are statements of specific, measurable changes within a defined time-frame.

Goals can clue the reader in on your highest motivations for proposing a program, but beware! Goals are no substitute for outcomes. Defining program outcomes is mandatory.

Example: A Goal and a Related Outcome

The results of the 2014 Youth Risk Behavior Survey revealed that 55% of the students at Douglas High School used alcohol regularly—a rate 15 percentage points higher than the statewide average of 40%. In response, the school developed a plan to produce steady reductions in this problem. The first step in the plan is a one-year program called *You Use, You Lose*, which is designed to help teens comprehend the dangers of using alcohol.

In this example the goal and outcome might look like this:

> **Goal:** *Students of Douglas High School will lead healthy, productive lives and will choose not to abuse alcohol.*
>
> **Outcome:** *Douglas High School's 2015 Youth Risk Behavior Survey results will show that the percentage of students who regularly use alcohol has decreased by ten percentage points: from 55% of the student body (550 students) in 2014, to 45% (450 students) in 2015.*

Beware of Awareness

Some people will argue that an increase in awareness counts as a meaningful outcome. But increased awareness is a huge "who cares?" It doesn't guarantee behavior change. People know that smoking is dangerous, but many continue to smoke.

People understand the benefits of exercise, yet many don't do it. Even if awareness motivates change, increased awareness is not an outcome because it is not a change in the problem itself.

For example, consider a community in which childhood obesity is a problem. In response to this problem, the Family Center is creating a program to decrease children's consumption of junk food. The center has learned that changing children's eating habits requires help from parents. It has also learned that parents won't be motivated to help if they're unaware of the dangers of childhood obesity and how junk food contributes to it. What if the Family Center's grant proposal includes the following outcome?

> *120 of the 180 parents who complete the Family Center's three-month parent education series will demonstrate increased:*
>
> * *knowledge of the dangers of childhood obesity*
> * *ability to identify junk food*
> * *understanding of how junk food contributes to obesity.*
>
> *The post-class Healthy Life Survey scores of 120 parents will be 70% higher than their pre-class scores on the survey.*

This outcome is meaningful only if the Family Center has documented that parents don't understand the perils of childhood obesity, can't tell the difference between junk food and healthy food, and don't understand the link between junk food and obesity. But even so, a reader is likely to say, "So what?" If increasing parental awareness doesn't cause children to eat less junk food, then what's the point?

If the purpose of the program is to decrease children's consumption of junk food, then another outcome must be added:

> *Of the estimated 423 children whose parents complete the parent education series, approximately 228 (54%) will significantly reduce junk food consumption. Nine months after the end of the parent education series, the Junk Food Tracker system will document that children whose parents increased their survey scores by at least 70% have, on average, reduced junk food intake by 50%–from approximately 14,000 to 7,000 calories per week.*

TWO EXCEPTIONS

Only two types of grant proposals can legitimately include increased awareness as an outcome:

- programs intended to stop a problem from occurring in the first place
- programs that won't produce measurable results in the problem until after the grant period ends.

But even in these cases, increased awareness can be a meaningful outcome only if research confirms that lack of awareness is a cause of the problem being addressed.

Prevention Programs & Delayed Outcomes

Some programs are designed to prevent problems from ever occurring—for example, substance abuse prevention programs. Other programs are designed to produce changes that will be realized only long after the program ends. A two-year program to reduce sources of pollution might not yield measurable changes in the affected lake until five years after the program ends.

But all proposals must define realistic and meaningful outcomes that can be measured during the period of grant funding. When it's not possible to measure changes in the problem during the grant period, you must propose outcomes that reflect a change in the causes of the problem, rather than in the problem itself.

Doing this requires solid evidence of those causes or evidence of what will prevent the problem from occurring. Only that evidence will enable you to propose meaningful outcomes that can be achieved during the grant period.

In all proposals, the problem discussion must identify the causes of the problem. But in a prevention proposal, the bar is set higher. Check the discussion of the problem to be sure that the causes are supported by the highest possible level of proof, preferably by research findings.

Unless the connection between the problem and its causes is absolutely solid, an outcome proposing a change in those causes will seem flimsy. Without this direct connection, a reader will be inclined to dismiss the outcomes with a shrug or a "so what?"

What if four of five beaches in an island community are polluted? To prevent pollution of the only remaining clean beach, the community must figure out why the other beaches are polluted and then determine which of those causes threatens the clean beach. Once the risks are identified, then the community can design a program that will decrease threats to the clean beach. The outcomes will depend on the causes of the pollution. Outcomes could be changes such as decreased permits for new construction within 100 feet of the beach, or increased stability of sand dunes, or a decrease in the number of tons of garbage dumped into the ocean.

EXAMPLES: OUTCOMES

EXAMPLE 1: Let's Read Together

Administrators at Franklin Elementary School are concerned because fifth graders are performing poorly on reading tests. Of the 280 fifth graders, 70 (25%) are reading at a third-grade level. The school designs a corrective program called *Let's Read Together*, applies for a state grant, and predicts this outcome:

> *Of the fifth graders at Franklin Elementary School, 50% of those who perform poorly on reading tests will increase their reading skills by 40% within six months.*

Sorry, but there are too many unanswered questions. The outcome says 50% of the students will benefit, but the percentage is meaningless unless the number is also stated. And without providing a baseline measurement of reading skills, it's impossible to know what a "40% improvement" means. Even though the outcome statement contains numbers, it's not useful.

Here's an improved version of the same outcome:

> *Of the 70 fifth graders at Franklin Elementary School who read at third-grade level, 21 (or 30%) will increase their reading skills by two grade levels within six months, as measured by the state's standard achievement test for reading.*

Use the checklist at the end of this chapter to make sure you include the necessary information in outcome statements by answering these five essential questions:

Who will change as a result of the program? Franklin Elementary School fifth graders reading at third-grade level.

How many will change? Twenty-one, or 30% of the 70 fifth graders now reading at third-grade level.

What type of change will take place? Children will improve their reading skills.

How much change will take place? Children will advance two grade levels in reading, from third- to fifth-grade level.

When will the change take place? Within six months of program start-up.

EXAMPLE 2: Improve the Response

A small police department trying to cover a large rural area has a problem: Its average response time when answering calls is too slow, endangering public safety. An analysis shows that the main cause for the slow response is that officers return to the station when they're on duty to file electronic reports after each incident. While back at the station, working on reports, officers are out of their assigned patrol areas, so it takes more time to get to people who call for help. When officers wait until their shifts end to file reports, they end up working overtime, straining the department's budget.

The department designs a program to address both concerns and applies for a state law enforcement grant. The outcomes they propose on the following page are right on the mark.

1. *Within three months of project implementation, department incident logs will document that the average response time to calls for assistance has decreased from 15 minutes (the current average) to five minutes (recommended by the National Council for Public Safety).*

2. *The department's annual program and financial audit of July 2015 will document that overtime attributed to routine paperwork has decreased from 400 hours annually to no more than 50 hours annually.*

In recent years, the harassment of students from immigrant families has been on the rise at William Grant High School. Incidents have ranged from taunting and insults to physical attacks. This trend has coincided with a surge in the city's immigrant population.

A school survey found that a majority of students believe that most immigrants are in the United States illegally, have low educational levels, are unemployed, and rely on public assistance to support their families. They also believe that crime rates rise as immigrants enter the community.

The school designs the *I Am Your Neighbor* program to reduce harassment by correcting these misconceptions, each of which can be refuted by studies and data. The program takes an arts-based approach to help students understand the immigrant experience and the actual characteristics of immigrants.

In its 2014 proposal for a grant to finance the program, the school predicts three SMART program outcomes:

1. *By the end of the 2015 academic year, school records will document that the number of harassment incidents has decreased by at least 57%, from the current level of 47 to 20 or fewer.*

2. *At the end of that school year, 1,000 randomly selected students will complete a questionnaire. The predicted outcome is that 825 of those students (83%) will demonstrate the following knowledge:*

   - *Only 16% of immigrants in the state are undocumented.*

   - *84% of immigrants in the state have a high school diploma and 57% have attended college or have a college degree.*

   - *The crime rate in the William Grant service area has decreased annually for the last ten years.*

   - *The percentage of immigrants in the state workforce is 67%, slightly higher than the percentage of non-immigrants.*

3. *Seven hundred (70%) of the 1,000 students who complete the questionnaire:*

3. Seven hundred (70%) of the 1,000 students who complete the questionnaire:

- *Will be able to cite three reasons immigrants come to this area.*

- *Will be able to cite two examples of how immigrants have enriched the city's business community, its arts or culture, or its educational system.*

EXAMPLE 4: The Bright Smiles Program

A health clinic is concerned about the incidence of tooth decay in students at a rural elementary school and has designed a three-year prevention program. This program is based on solid research showing that when parents provide good oral hygiene care to infants and then help their children practice good oral hygiene as toddlers, the children are likely to continue good habits resulting in less tooth decay by the time they enter elementary school.

The clinic's *Bright Smiles Program* will address two issues identified as pivotal causes of tooth decay in young children: inadequate oral hygiene and the use of milk or sweet fluids in overnight bottles. An earlier section of the grant proposal established that these two behaviors are primary contributors to childhood tooth decay. That proven connection between the behaviors and the decay is what makes the program outcomes meaningful.

The *Bright Smiles Program* will provide three years of service to children who are now infants and to their parents. The program's goal and long-term outcome are based on research showing that the positive tooth-care habits a family develops during the first three years of a child's life will continue. Because of that research, the clinic predicts that when infants whose families participated in the program enter first grade in 2021, they will have good oral health. The outcomes predict the specific and measurable changes that will take place during the three-year grant period.

> *Goal and Outcomes for the Bright Smiles Program*
>
> *Goal: Children in Chester County will have good oral health—strong teeth and bright smiles.*
>
> *Long-Term Outcome: Children in the Jason Elementary School first-grade class of 2021 will have better oral health than classes in previous years. Currently, the in-school dental clinic diagnoses approximately 140 of the 200 first graders (70% of the class) with childhood tooth decay each year. In six years, when the class of 2021 enters first grade, the school clinic will document that 70 or fewer of the 200 first graders have tooth decay—a decrease of at least 50% from the current average.*

Outcomes:

1. *Within two months of beginning the Bright Smiles Program, 100 of the 150 parents who had not cleaned their children's gums or teeth regularly will report that they are cleaning their infants' gums or helping toddlers brush their teeth twice each day, in the morning and again before bed.*

2. *Within two months of beginning the Bright Smiles Program, 75 of the 100 parents who reported that they put their children to bed each night with a bottle of milk or juice will report that they now use only water.*

3. *At the end of three years, 75 of the 150 parents participating in the Bright Smiles Program will report that they are continuing good oral hygiene habits: (a) toddlers' teeth are brushed in the morning and at night; and (b) overnight bottles and before-bed drinks contain only water instead of milk or sweet fluids.*

CHECKLIST: OUTCOMES

☐   1. Define outcomes that are specific and measurable.

☐   2. Define outcomes that are achievable and reasonable.

☐   3. Describe who or what will change as a result of the program.

☐   4. Specify how many will change.

☐   5. Describe the type of change that will take place.

☐   6. Define how much change will take place.

☐   7. Define the time frame in which the change will take place.

☐   8. Do not describe methods or the quantity of service to be provided by a program.

☐   9. May briefly note how the change will be documented.

☐ 10. Are written in positive and declarative language.

Though this be madness,
yet there is method in it.

WILLIAM SHAKESPEARE

Hamlet

Methods
What Activities Will You Use?

So far, you've introduced your organization, identified the problem it's concerned about, and described the outcomes you expect your program to produce. Now it's time to explain how your organization will produce those outcomes.

Before sorting out which methods will be most effective, it's crucial to identify what's causing the problem. Only when you understand why the problem exists can your organization decide what steps to take. For example, if children are having trouble reading, the first question to ask is "why?" If they read poorly because they're hungry, then a school breakfast program makes more sense than computer-assisted instruction.

Overview & Rationale

Starting with an overview will keep reviewers from getting lost in the details of this section. If the methods will include several major categories of activity, list them in the overview before you begin a detailed explanation of each.

Explain why your organization selected the approach you plan to use and why you

expect it to work. Sometimes the choice of a method may seem obvious. If a stream is polluted because a factory is violating environmental laws, the best method to improve the situation may be simply to enforce existing laws. But what's obvious to the proposal writer may not be clear to the proposal reader.

Your organization might select an approach because it relates well to the culture of the participants, or because it has produced good results in similar circumstances. Perhaps research studies have documented its effectiveness or it's the only approach acceptable to the community. Or it may be the most affordable option.

Some funders will support only projects that use proven methods. See the box on the next page for the hierarchy of proven approaches.

ELEMENTS OF THE METHODS SECTION

Overview & Rationale

Details of the Approach

- Beneficiaries & participants
- Major components of activity
- Staffing
- Facilities, equipment, & supplies

Timeline

A PROVEN APPROACH

These terms, used for methods that are supported by some degree of evidence, are listed from the least to the most rigorously tested.

Promising practice: an approach that has not been rigorously evaluated but is supported by anecdotal or modest evidence.

Best practice: an approach recognized by a profession as the best way to do something. These practices may or may not be evidence-based or science-based, but they are based on experience within a field.

Evidence-based approach: a method validated by substantial evidence derived from rigorous evaluation. This term may be used interchangeably with "proven approach."

Science-based approach: a method that has been evaluated with a high level of scientific rigor and statistical analysis, possibly using control groups and requiring results that can be replicated.

Who Will Benefit?
Who Will Participate?

Those who will participate in a program are not always the same as those who will benefit. For example, in a program to decrease pollution of a lake, the participants will be farmers who decrease the use of toxic chemicals. The beneficiaries will be the people who drink the lake water and use the lake for recreation.

If those who will participate are different from those who will benefit, be sure to describe both. Who and how many will participate, and who and how many will benefit?

Target population? Those who will benefit from a program are often called the "target population" and are described in the Problem Section. In the Methods Section, the target population must be even more thoroughly defined.

In the Methods Section, include such relevant details as the reading levels of students who will be tutored, the average blood sugar levels of diabetics who will change their diets, or the average weight of coyotes that will be relocated. Depending on the program, you might also need to discuss such things as age, income level, ethnicity, educational level, or native language.

If your program won't have the capacity to help everyone who needs it, explain the criteria you'll use to select participants and how you'll handle those who must be turned away. Will there be a waiting list? Will staff refer them to other services?

Voluntary or mandatory participation? When a school proposes a new first-grade reading curriculum, student participation will obviously be mandatory and there's no need to explain it. But what about remedial education for offenders? If it's voluntary, readers will wonder why the offenders will participate, and they'll want to see a realistic recruitment plan.

Collateral beneficiaries? Sometimes others, in addition to the target population, may benefit from a program. As sixth-graders who are lagging behind in reading improve their skills, the teacher can give more attention to other students. Mentioning secondary beneficiaries can strengthen your case for funding.

How many? A common mistake in grant proposals is describing the participants and beneficiaries, yet forgetting to tell the reviewer the numbers. How many will participate? How many will benefit?

Major Components of Activity

Because the Methods Section must provide a plethora of detail, organize it clearly and sort information into major components with subheadings. A program to clean up downtown may include four major components: volunteer recruitment, work crew supervision, refuse disposal, and community celebration.

Try to think like the funder, the person reading and evaluating your proposal. You may need to explain why an activity is necessary. Why is a Friday lunch crucial to the senior program? Why is one curriculum better than another?

Quantify What the Program Will Deliver

Some funders use the word "output" to refer to the quantity of service delivered during a set time period. Other funders use such terms as "process objectives" or simply "objectives." But whatever they call it, be sure to quantify exactly what the program will do.

Telling the reader how much, how many, and by when is a fundamental part of explaining the method. The term "benchmark" is sometimes used to refer to a specific accomplishment that will be achieved by a certain time. Statements that specifically quantify what will be accomplished and by when are more useful to the reader.

Vague Statement of Method	vs.	Output (Process Objective)
Children will be provided with tutoring services.		Each of the 50 children participating in the program will be provided with 15 hours of tutoring each month for six months.
Hospital employees will be trained in the new hand-washing procedure.		1,500 hospital employees will each receive two hours of training in the new hand-washing procedure within six months of program start-up.

Vague Accomplishment	vs.	Benchmark
Children will sign up for the tutoring program.		50 children will be enrolled in the tutoring program by January 15, 2016.
Hand-washing training sessions will be completed.		20 hand-washing training sessions will be scheduled during the first quarter.

Collaboration

Partners can bring needed expertise and substantial resources such as office space or a fleet of vans. They might even provide access to new funding streams to keep the program alive after the grant expires. If your organization will collaborate with others, funders will want to know what each organization will contribute and how the relationships will work.

Collaborations vary, but partners must be invested in the program and what it's working to accomplish, and they must be willing to participate in planning and reporting. Sometimes, in highly collaborative programs, partners are integral in decision-making and the applicant organization is the convener, facilitator, and administrator.

Collaborations can be powerful, but that doesn't mean they're easy. Because of this, it is essential to define relationships and responsibilities clearly.

When describing the collaboration, include the following information:

- the name and address of each collaborating organization
- the qualifications of each
- a description of the role and responsibilities of each
- a list of the resources each partner is committing
- for complex projects, a chart or written description of the lines of authority.

Unless application guidelines forbid it, a memorandum of understanding or a letter of commitment from each collaborating organization should be included as an attachment to the proposal.

Remember, no matter how many partners are involved, the applicant organization holds bottom-line responsibility for program operation and the management of grant funds.

Memoranda of understanding (MOUs) and letters of commitment. These documents detail the involvement and contributions of partner organizations. MOUs and letters of commitment represent obligations if the proposal is funded, so organizations take them seriously.

Once you know what each partner will be contributing, draft notes reflecting your understanding. Partners can use your notes to make sure their MOUs or letters confirm the relationships and roles that will be described in the Methods Section. And if you've misunderstood their commitment, your write-up can be a starting point for sorting things out.

Get an MOU or letter of commitment from each partner and be sure they're signed by people with the authority to commit the collaborators to their roles. Typically, letters should be addressed to the executive director of the applicant organization, not to the funder.

The written commitment of partners can provide powerful quotes for the Methods Section. Don't simply say, "Many community organizations are committed to this program. (See attached letters.)" Instead, insert a couple of good quotes and then say, "See attached letters."

MEMORANDA OF UNDERSTANDING & LETTERS OF COMMITMENT

- express intent to provide assistance to the program
- are specific about what each partner will provide
- confirm the relationships and commitments described in the Methods Section
- are signed by people in a position to make the commitments
- are essential to credibility when the program includes contributions from others.

When a funder restricts the number of attachments that can accompany a proposal, you may be unable to submit an individual letter from each collaborator. In this situation, compose one document that briefly spells out each commitment and provides a signature line for each collaborator. Because the document must be signed by an authorized representative of each organization, the process can be a logistical nightmare. Allow plenty of time for completing it.

Staffing

After you've explained what your organization plans to do, tell the reader who will do it—who will implement those activities. Describe staff roles, responsibilities, and qualifications. Tell the reader if positions will be full-time or a percentage of full-time and how long they'll last. Six months? Two years?

If you identify a specific individual for a key role, explain why that person's experience and education are a good fit for the position. When staff will be hired, describe the required qualifications.

Job descriptions and résumés are often required. Follow funder guidelines on whether to summarize them in the text of the proposal or make them separate attachments. When there are no instructions, attach them.

In complex projects, it's wise to include an organizational chart depicting lines of authority. An understanding of the chain of command helps readers see how a program will operate.

Volunteers

Enlisting volunteers demonstrates community support and can expand a program's capacity. But volunteers come and go; they're a somewhat fluid resource. It's important to consider volunteer involvement carefully and to put necessary systems in place to support them.

If volunteers will play a major role, explain:

- the skills and qualifications required
- how they'll be recruited
- the screening and selection criteria
- how they'll be trained and supervised
- the expected duration of their service
- how your organization will acknowledge their contributions.

Facilities, Equipment, & Supplies

The physical support required for operating programs varies tremendously. For example, an after-school arts program may have access to a school classroom, a computer, and a color printer at no cost. The only expense may be $2,500 each semester to pay for ink cartridges, paper, paint, chalks, and other materials.

On the other hand, a cardiovascular-health program that will include screening for heart disease may require a mobile laboratory, various pieces of medical equipment, supplies for drawing and screening blood samples, and brochures printed in several languages.

In all cases, facilities must be appropriate, safe, and accessible for those who participate. If existing facilities and equipment will be used, describe them and provide assurances that they will be available. When new facilities or equipment are required, describe what's needed and why. Is a high-end computer a must for the program's graphic-design component, or would a less expensive one do the job?

Timeline

A timeline chart is helpful for both the applicant and the reviewer. It's a good check for making sure the Methods Section includes all of the necessary steps, and it's a good management tool once you receive a grant. It can also give a funder confidence in the program by showing that you've thought things through and have a logical plan of action.

A timeline organizes major program activities, showing when each will occur and who is responsible.

To construct a timeline:

1. Identify primary activities required to implement all program components.

2. Determine the sequence of activities.

3. Determine who will implement each activity.

4. Estimate the time needed to complete each activity.

5. Transfer the information onto a chart.

Timeline formats can vary. Examples are included at the end of this chapter.

Aligning the Methods & the Budget

The budget and the methods must correlate. The activities and resources (personnel, space, equipment, and supplies) discussed in one section must show up in the other as well. If the Methods Section mentions a van for transporting senior citizens, then the Budget Section must include it as a donated resource or an expense covered by the grant. And if the Budget Section includes an administrative assistant, the Methods Section must mention that position and its contribution to the program. Readers often scan the budget to increase their understanding of the program design. When the methods and the budget don't align, it creates confusion and the proposal loses credibility.

What's Plan B?

Plans don't always turn out as we expect. Consider whether the proposed program runs the risk of encountering substantial obstacles. If so, including a Plan B in your proposal may be a good idea. But do this only when the potential barriers are so apparent that a funder might look at the proposal and think, "Whoaooo, what if….?" When your organization is prepared for a curveball or two, the funder is more likely to be comfortable and the program is more likely to succeed.

Pilot, Demonstration, & Model Programs

Some programs offer the possibility of benefits that reach far beyond the people immediately involved. Although they deliver service to a particular community, the primary purpose of a pilot, demonstration, or model program is to determine the effectiveness of specific approaches— to gain new knowledge that will enrich the field.

If a large national funder focuses on innovation, it may show little interest in a proposal for a small, localized mentoring program. But if the approach is new, appears promising, will include a rigorous evaluation, and could be useful to others in the field, the funder may be more interested.

Although the terminology is somewhat changeable, these definitions should be helpful:

- **Pilot programs** are small-scale ventures that examine new approaches in order to determine whether larger-scale demonstrations are warranted.

- **Demonstration programs** test the applicability of promising research findings, explore whether small pilot projects can be successful on a larger scale, or examine whether an approach that has been successful in one environment or with one specific group of participants will be effective elsewhere or with other types of participants.

- **Model programs** may be evidence-based programs that have proven successful in achieving a specific result. But this term is also used for promising new approaches that planners expect others to emulate. When used in this context, "model program" is synonymous with what some funders call an "innovative program."

Before declaring that a program is a worthy approach that has not yet been tried, be sure the claim is true. Do your homework and know the field. If the program does represent a new approach, explain why it should be expected to work. Does it combine several science-based approaches in a way never before tried? Is it based on reputable new research that hasn't yet been tested? What's innovative and why is it likely to succeed?

Logic Models

A flowchart or graphic that presents the rationale for the program plan is called a logic model. It shows how methods and outcomes are connected. A quick search of the Internet will produce lots of examples from universities, foundations, government agencies, and others.

Although some funders request a logic model and leave the rest to you, others use specific formats and require applicants to follow their directions. If you've studied the funder's information carefully and you still don't understand the terms used or the concepts represented in the logic model, contact the funder for clarification.

Here's the structure of a typical logic model:

Inputs	Activities	Outputs	Outcomes	Impact
Resources such as staffing, participants, funding, facilities, equipment, & supplies	Major tasks that the program will complete	Specific types & quantities of services to be delivered within set time frames	Results: expected changes in behaviors, skills, knowledge, or circumstances (also called program objectives or short-term impact)	The long-term change to which the outcomes will contribute; usually not measurable within grant period (also called long-term impact or goal)

Understanding each proposal component described in this book will help you deal with different logic model formats. Although the terminology used by funders is often different, the basic concepts are the same.

Typical Logic Model Terms	Other Terms Funders May Use	Where to find this concept in The Grantsmanship Center Model
Inputs	Resources	The Methods Section describes participants, staffing, collaborators, facilities, equipment, and supplies. The Budget Section defines both cash and in-kind resources.
Activities	Approach Strategies	The Methods Section identifies major components of the program approach.
Outputs	Benchmarks Objectives Process objectives	The Methods Section defines the types and quantities of activity that are planned.
Outcomes	Results Goals Objectives Program outcomes Outcome objectives Short-term impact	The Outcomes Section defines the specific, measurable results the program is expected to produce.
Impact	Results Goal Long-term impact	When long-term impact is defined, that information will be in the Outcomes Section.

EXAMPLES: METHODS

EXAMPLE 1: Hands Against Infection Program (HAIP)

Administrators at Hometown Hospital are concerned because patients suffer a high rate of secondary infections. After investigation, they conclude that inadequate hand washing by hospital personnel is the primary cause. To reduce infections, they will implement more effective hand-washing procedures.

The one-year Hands Against Infection Program *will establish more effective hand-washing procedures within Hometown Hospital. All approaches are based on results from similar efforts in ten comparable hospitals and on recommendations of the National Council to Reduce Hospital Infections. (See attached bibliography.) The program will include four major components: (1) establishing the Hands Against Infection team; (2) identifying more effective hand-washing procedures; (3) educating staff and volunteers; and (4) monitoring and enforcing compliance.*

Target Population & Program Participants

All 1,500 hospital employees and 300 volunteers (1,800 personnel total) will be required to participate in the program. Full participation will result in fewer secondary infections among our target population, the 100,000 patients Hometown Hospital serves each year.

Patient demographics reflect the general population of the service area described in the Introduction Section: they are predominantly middle income, 28% are minorities, and there are slightly more women than men (52% vs 48%). Approximately 17.5% of patients are under age 18, 26% are age 18 to 44, 23% are age 45-64, and 33.5% are over age 65.

Of the 1,500 employees who will participate in the Hands Against Infection Program, 650 are medical staff and 850 are nonmedical staff. All 300 volunteers perform nonmedical services.

In addition to reducing secondary infections among patients, we also expect the program to produce such ancillary benefits as healthier employees and reduced operating costs.

Program Components

1. Establishing the Team

A 12-member interdisciplinary team of hospital employees will guide program implementation. This team will make recommendations and also conduct employee training.

Dr. Jun Wong, Director of Research, will ask department supervisors to recommend staff. After considering each nominee's leadership skills and potential as a trainer, Dr. Wong will select four doctors, four nurses, and four senior administrative staff for the team. The diverse experience of members will help to create practical, effective procedures and a realistic enforcement approach. Members will be given 30% (1.5 days per week) release time from their regular duties for six months.

2. Identifying More Effective Procedures

The National Council to Reduce Hospital Infections recommends five science-based hand-washing procedures. Each has merit and presents particular implementation challenges. The Hands Against Infection team will: (a) review each procedure for compatibility with existing hospital procedures; (b) examine reports on implementation and outcomes of the five procedures at hospitals of similar size; and (c) make site visits to hospitals or bring in experts from other hospitals, as needed.

After considering the five potential procedures, the team will recommend an approach for Hometown Hospital. Dr. Wong will mediate the decision-making. The team will justify its recommendation in a report requesting approval from the Hospital Improvement Committee.

3. Educating Employees

Establishing new hand-washing procedures requires employee education along with follow-up reminders (Infection Control Report, U.S. Health Research Council, 2014). Therefore, this program includes 1.5 hours of training for hospital personnel, followed by regular reminders.

The hospital's employees and volunteers will be sorted into the following categories for training based on the type of contact they have with patients: (1) doctors; (2) other medical staff; and (3) nonmedical staff.

Vera Martinez, M.D., consultant to the program, will design a 1.5-hour training curriculum for each personnel category. The 2014 U.S. Health Research Council report documented that 1.5-hour training sessions are optimal for educating personnel about hand-washing procedures. Dr. Martinez will also develop a five-hour train-the-trainer curriculum for preparing the Hands Against Infection team to train other personnel. Dr. Wong will oversee the work of Dr. Martinez.

After they are prepared, each team member will lead five training sessions, each of which will include approximately 30 participants. Dr. Martinez will provide support and supervision. All staff and volunteers will be trained within a six-week period. Once current personnel have been trained, the team will train new personnel weekly.

At the conclusion of each training, participants will complete feedback forms. Dr. Martinez will develop the form and will evaluate the feedback. She will then collaborate with the team to determine how trainings can be improved.

Paul Justice, Director of Communications, will work with Dr. Martinez to develop a brochure for each personnel category to supplement the training. He will produce the brochures in various languages as needed.

The National Council to Reduce Hospital Infections states that ongoing reminders are critical in promoting compliance with new procedures (Infection Prevention Newsletter #28, November 2014). Paul Justice will design a reminder system that will include emails, posters, handouts for departmental staff meetings, and advertisements in employee and volunteer newsletters. The system will include a minimum of eight reminders per month for each personnel category.

4. Monitoring and Enforcing Compliance

To ensure sensitive and realistic enforcement approaches, the Hands Against Infection team will consult with department supervisors and will then make recommendations to the Hospital Improvement Committee. Each of the hospital's 15 department supervisors will be responsible for enforcing compliance.

The firm of T&K Black, Inc. will conduct the evaluation, including technology upgrades and data collection. The firm will provide an interim implementation report in month seven, and a full evaluation report in month 12 that analyzes both implementation and patient outcomes. The full evaluation plan begins on page 15.

STAFFING PLAN: Hands Against Infection Program (HAIP)

Role; Responsible Party; Time on HAIP	Qualifications (résumés attached)	Responsibilities (job descriptions attached)	Status & Funding
HAIP leader; Dr. Jun Wong; 30% FTE, 1 yr	M.D., Ivy Medical School; 20 yrs administration at hospital; 2 yrs on National Council to Reduce Hospital Infections	Select & manage HAIP team; supervise consultants & communication campaign	On staff; time donated by hospital
HAIP team; 4 doctors, 4 nurses, 4 senior staff; 30% FTE, 6 months	Leadership skills; ability to train other staff; commitment to reducing infection	Recommend hand-washing procedures, monitoring methods, & enforcement approach; train other staff	On staff; time donated by hospital
Communications director; Paul Justice; 30% FTE 1 yr, then 10% FTE	M.A., communication; 30 yrs experience in public education & writing	Produce instructional brochures; design & implement reminder system	On staff; time donated by hospital
Department supervisors; 15 senior staff; 5% FTE, ongoing	Advanced degrees and health-care experience	Implement HAIP monitoring and enforcement	On staff; time donated by hospital
Training consultant; Dr. Vera Martinez; 400 hours over 1 yr	M.D., Prestige Medical School; 20 yrs infection control specialty; 10 yrs national trainer	Design training curricula; train team & mentor team members; revise training as needed	Contracted upon grant award; paid by grant
Evaluation consultant; T&K Black, Inc.; 1-yr contract	Top medical evaluation firm; similar work at 15 hospitals	Implement evaluation; report on outcomes (see evaluation plan, page 15)	Contracted upon grant award; paid by grant

TIMELINE: Hands Against Infection Program Implementation

Tasks	Who is Responsible	When
Finalize contracts with T&K Black, Inc. & Dr. V. Martinez	Dr. Wong	Month 1
Confirm baseline data against which improvement will be measured	T&K Black, Inc.	Months 1-2
Select HAIP Team: 4 doctors, 4 nurses, & 4 senior staff	Dr. Wong	Month 1
Examine hand-washing procedures approved by National Council to Reduce Hospital Infections	Dr. Wong & HAIP team	Months 2-3
Recommend procedures & methods for monitoring & enforcement	Dr. Wong & HAIP team	Month 3
Obtain approval of Hospital Improvement Committee for procedures & methods for monitoring & enforcement	Dr. Wong	Month 3
Create training curricula for procedures & train-the-trainer curriculum for HAIP Team	Dr. Martinez	Month 4
Prepare HAIP team to teach curricula to hospital staff	Dr. Martinez	Month 4
Prepare instructional brochures for procedures	Paul Justice	Month 4
Distribute brochures to staff	HAIP team	Months 5-6
Train doctors on procedures	HAIP team	Month 5
Train other medical staff on procedures	HAIP team	Month 5
Train nonmedical staff on procedures	HAIP team	Month 6
Monitor & enforce hand-washing procedures	Department supervisors	Begin month 6
Implement reminder system	Paul Justice	Begin month 6
Prepare for & conduct project evaluation	T&K Black, Inc.	Months 1-12
Evaluation report delivered to Hospital Improvement Committee and Board of Directors	Dr. Wong & T&K Black, Inc.	Month 7 & Month 12

LOGIC MODEL: Hands Against Infection Program

Inputs	Activities	Outputs	Outcomes	Impact
• 13 employees • 15 supervisors • communication specialist • consultant expert • evaluation firm • 1,800 personnel • 6 training rooms • clerical support • printing services • $250K grant	• identify better procedures • develop training • develop brochures • train personnel • remind personnel • enforce procedures • evaluate procedures	**By month 6:** • new procedures in place • 1,800 personnel trained • brochures to all personnel • 8 reminders/ month per category **Evaluation Reports** • midway, month 7 • final, month 12	• 95% compliance by month 7 • data for months 7-12 show 50% decrease from current 6-month average of secondary infections (from 120 to 60 patients)	• fewer complications & deaths from secondary infections • average hospital stay reduced • financial savings to hospital & patients

EXAMPLE 2: Parent Stress-Reduction Program

In response to local data showing that postpartum stress can contribute to child abuse, a family center in Mill City, Kansas, is planning a stress-reduction program. Data published by the State Agency of Child Protection showed that, without intervention, 40% of mothers who have a newborn and who have previously been charged with abuse will mistreat their children again during the postpartum period. In this program, the criteria for selecting participants are critical.

> *The one-year* Parent Stress-Reduction Program *will work to reduce child abuse. All aspects of the program will comply with the Stop Abuse Now (SAN) program model and curriculum developed by the National Abuse Prevention Council. When this model is implemented with fidelity, an 80% success rate can be expected (Stop Abuse Now Evaluation Report, Abuse Prevention Center, 2014).*
>
> *The program will have three components: (1) assessing the needs of parents referred to the program; (2) implementing Parent Stress-Reduction classes; and (3) providing parent support.*
>
> ### Target Population
>
> *The purpose of the program is to protect a minimum of 100 children in Mill City, Kansas, who are at elevated risk for abuse. Participating parents will also benefit from increased coping skills and ongoing support to increase family stability.*
>
> *The State Agency of Child Protection (the Agency) will be the program's sole referral source. To be referred, parents must meet all of the following criteria: (1) have a newborn who is less than six months old; (2) have previously abused another child; and (3) have one or more children living at home who are under the legal guardianship of the state. In two-parent households, both parents will be expected to participate.*
>
> *From a review of agency data, we estimate that the program will serve 56 parents, representing 40 families, including:*
> * *24 single parents*
> * *30 families below the poverty level*
> * *Parents ranging from 16 to 42 years old*
> * *Children from newborn to 16 years old*

We anticipate that half of the parents will have two children and half will have three or more children, so that altogether the program will work to protect approximately 100 or more children.

The Agency will direct referred parents to participate in the program. Parents who refuse to participate will have more frequent home reviews and more stringent reporting mandates. Agency home-review procedures and reporting mandates are attached.

The program will accept referrals on a first-come, first-served basis. If more parents are referred than can be served, the Family Center will establish a waiting list and seek funding to add more groups.

Major Components of the Parent Stress-Reduction Program

1. Assessing Parent Needs

Each parent referred to the program will be assigned to one of the program's two licensed mental health counselors. The counselors will meet with parents individually to discuss the program, complete paperwork, plan for additional counseling and family support services, and make referrals to additional services if needed.

2. Parent Stress-Reduction Classes

Each class will include a maximum of 20 parents, last two hours, meet twice a week for six months, and include an informal meal. The Family Center will provide child care and arrange transportation to and from classes if needed.

The Program's two counselors will co-facilitate all class sessions. Each counselor is experienced in child-abuse prevention and intervention.

Over the course of 52 group meetings, parents will learn stress-reduction and relaxation techniques, learn and practice anger management and nonviolent communication, learn about child development, explore community resources that can assist their families, participate in low-cost or free recreation, and discuss the long-term impact of child abuse. The Stop Abuse Now curriculum summary is attached.

3. Parent Support

The program's two counselors will provide parent support services and will refer families to the Center's clinical counseling program or other additional resources as needed.

During the six-month class period, program counselors will provide individualized support services through monthly home visits to each family. For three months after the classes end, parents will meet with a program counselor once a week for ongoing support. Meetings may be held at the Center or in the family's home. Parents in the program can also call the Family Center's crisis line, which connects parents to on-call clinical counselors 24 hours a day, seven days a week.

After the year of training and support, parents will be encouraged to use the Center as an ongoing resource.

Staffing

The Parent Stress-Reduction Program will be staffed by two full-time employees.

Anna Tartok will direct the program. Dr. Tartok holds a master's degree in family counseling and a Ph.D. in psychology. She is a licensed mental health counselor. Prior to joining the Family Center, Dr. Tartok directed the Family Services Center of the Central Kansas Mental Health Agency for eight years, and served as a family counselor for four years in the Central Kansas Medical Center's Behavioral Health Program. As director, Dr. Tartok will serve as the primary liaison with the State Agency of Child Protection, will ensure all program components are implemented as planned, will be responsible for program reporting, and will receive direct supervision from the executive director of the Family Center.

Jackson Frisno will serve as senior counselor for the program. Mr. Frisno holds a master's degree in psychology and family counseling and is a licensed mental health counselor. Prior to joining the Family Center, Mr. Frisno served as an intervention counselor for the State Child Protection Agency for five years, and operated a private family counseling service for four years. Mr. Frisno will assist Dr. Tartok in all areas of program implementation. Mr. Frisno will receive direct supervision from Dr. Tartok.

Within one month of the grant award, Dr. Tartok and Mr. Frisno will participate in 40 hours of training on the Stop Abuse Now (SAN) curriculum. Dr. Lenore Jervison, a certified instructor of this curriculum, will provide the training. (See letter of commitment and résumé in the appendix.) The Family Center will also contract with Dr. Jervison for ongoing technical assistance in implementing the program model.

Dr. Tartok and Mr. Frisno will both conduct assessments, deliver the curriculum, provide family support, and make referrals. Job descriptions and résumés are in the appendix.

Facilities, Equipment, and Supplies

The Family Center is located in downtown Mill City at 110 Main Street. In addition to a dedicated family-friendly waiting area, our facility includes staff offices, two conference rooms, and ten private counseling rooms. The Family Center has abundant free parking in a lot immediately adjacent to our facility and is on two major city bus lines. The Family Center facility will be used for assessments and individual support and counseling.

The Tanglewood Unitarian Church is located next door to the Family Center at 108 Main Street. The Center frequently uses the church's community rooms to operate training programs and events. The church membership is committed to the Parent Stress-Reduction Program and will provide free use of its community rooms for the program's parent training classes, child care, and meals. A letter of commitment is attached.

The Family Center and the Unitarian Church both have large inventories of toys and child development equipment that will be used in the program. The church also maintains a fully equipped kitchen that it will make available to the program. (See attached letter.)

In addition to standard, consumable office supplies, the program will need to purchase curriculum materials for program staff and for participating families. Those costs are detailed in the line-item budget and budget narrative. Both staff members will use Family Center computers, printers, and other equipment as needed.

TIMELINE: Parent Stress-Reduction Program

Major Task	Month											
	1	2	3	4	5	6	7	8	9	10	11	12
Reassign Dr. Tartok & Mr. Frisno to program	X											
Stop Abuse Now (SAN) training	X											
Technical assistance in SAN implementation	Month 1 and ongoing											
Confirm plans with the Agency	X											
Accept referrals from the Agency		X	X									
Conduct family assessments		X	X									
Conduct SAN classes				6 months of classes								
Monthly support meeting w/ each family				6 months of family meetings								
Weekly support meeting w/ each family										3 months		
Refer families to clinical counseling & additional supports		Month 2 and ongoing										
Provide implementation reports to the Agency			X			X			X			X
Assess effectiveness & plan for coming year											X	X

EXAMPLE 3: Environmental Advocacy Program for the Swift River

The water quality of the Swift River is threatened by a planned residential and commercial development of forest and farmland along its banks. The developer is the Rupin Corporation; the land in question is known as the Burton Estate. A study by the State University Environmental Laboratory has concluded that development of the estate's land poses a significant threat to the river's water quality. The finding is alarming because the river is the primary source of drinking water for cities and towns in the area. Save Our River has devised an environmental advocacy program to stop the development, and is asking the River Watch Foundation for funding to support staff work. Save Our River has also assembled a group of allied organizations that are contributing their services to this effort.

The Rupin Corporation is having difficulty obtaining financing to develop the Burton Estate. This has delayed negotiations with the Burton family and gives Save Our River time to intervene. This 14-month project will prevent the proposed development and will help preserve the Burton Estate for future generations.

Save Our River will collaborate with the seven allied organizations described in the Introduction Section of this proposal: Swift RiverKeeper, Conserve Our Land, Farmsteads Unite, State Environmental Coalition, State Department of Parks, and local chapters of both Protect the Earth and Wildlife Guardians. These organizations helped plan the project and will provide crucial expertise and resources. Letters of commitment are attached.

The 1.5 million people living in the Swift River watershed will benefit from this project, especially the 900,000 who depend on the river for drinking water.

Three-part Plan to Stop the Rupin Corporation's Development

   1. Oppose Rezoning Request
   Rupin has filed with Titan County for rezoning of the Burton Estate from agricultural to residential/mixed use. Swift RiverKeeper and Protect the Earth will join Save Our River to oppose this request. Save Our River has succeeded in similar efforts, and our allied organizations have a large number of active members who will help block this zoning change.

   2. Include Burton Property in Wetlands Inventory
   Wildlife Guardians will join Save Our River to advocate that wetlands on the estate be added to the Swift River System Wetlands Inventory. Once the

3333

333

333333

wetlands are included in the inventory, it will be difficult for any developer to obtain and file the necessary permits for development.

3. Amend Storm Water Regulations

The State Environmental Coalition and Save Our River will propose amendments to storm water regulations now being updated by the State Environmental Protection Agency. These amendments will require that new developments exceeding 350 acres construct storm water treatment plants with effluent standards equal to state sewage treatment facilities. Adoption of these amendments will significantly increase the cost of Rupin's project and discourage the development of the Burton Estate.

Two-part Plan to Preserve the Estate for the Future

Save Our River will work with allied organizations to establish a state park on the forested portion of the Burton Estate and to preserve the estate's open land as a working farm.

1. Establishing a State Park

The State Department of Parks has identified the 10,375 forested acres of the Burton Estate as an optimal site for establishing a park in the Swift River watershed. Because of an unexpected budget shortfall, the Department's plans to purchase the property have been placed on hold.

Our partner, Conserve Our Land, has a successful track record of fundraising to acquire environmentally valuable land, then purchasing and holding the land until government agencies can buy and preserve it. Conserve Our Land will organize and lead the fundraising effort to purchase the forested portion of the Burton Estate.

Save Our River will negotiate an agreement between Conserve Our Land and the Department of Parks spelling out: (a) the intent of Conserve Our Land to purchase and hold the forested portion of the estate until the Department of Parks can acquire it; and (b) the intent of the Department of Parks to acquire the property for a state park. The Burton family has demonstrated commitment to Save Our River through its financial support and by providing a site for the Save Our River picnics. Save Our River will serve as the liaison with the family to help Conserve Our Land secure a right of first refusal to purchase the forested portion of the estate.

Farming is a part of the Burton family heritage, and the 3,900 non-forested acres of the estate are an active farm. Save Our River is working with the State Department of Agriculture to determine whether farmland preservation subsidies could compensate the family for easements that would permanently prohibit development of the farm. We are also consulting with the family attorney regarding possible tax benefits for the family if easements are instituted. Save Our River will serve as the liaison with the family to help Farmsteads Unite negotiate perpetual conservation easements. Once established, Farmsteads Unite will monitor and enforce the easements.

Project Staffing

This section notes the percentage of time staff will dedicate to this 14-month project and briefly describes qualifications and roles. Job descriptions and résumés are in the appendix.

***Executive Director, Mackenzi Okeke (20%)**, has a B.S. in environmental studies, M.B.A. in nonprofit management and 20 years experience in environmental advocacy. She will serve as lead spokesperson, supervise Save Our River (SOR) staff, engage SOR board, serve as liaison with allied organizations and the Burton family, and assist in fundraising.*

***Burton Project Director, Eric Wilson (100%)**, has an M.S., in environmental management and ten years experience managing land preservation projects. He will lead strategy development, manage implementation, coordinate efforts of board, staff, and allied organizations, provide information for legal briefs and public communications, and prepare reports.*

***Legal Director, Chris Ng (30%)**, holds a J.D. and has practiced environmental law for 15 years. He will draft legal documents and proposed regulations, help develop and implement strategy, and assist in all negotiations.*

***Communications Director, Nancy Gonzalez (15%)**, holds an M.A. in journalism and has eight years experience as communications director for environmental advocacy groups. She will develop communication strategies, prepare board and staff for presentations, respond to media inquiries, prepare advocacy materials, serve as a spokesperson, and prepare fundraising materials.*

Board Chair, Peter Simmons (2%), *holds a J.D. and is partner in Wilcox & Simmons, LLC. He will present project strategy to the board, serve as liaison with boards of allied organizations, and represent Save Our River with government agencies and the Burton family.*

Conserve Our Land *will contribute staff necessary to lead all fundraising for purchase of the forested portion of the estate. A letter of commitment and fundraising plan synopsis are in the appendix.*

Facilities and Supplies

Save Our River will contribute office space, equipment, and supplies for this project.

Timeline

This timeline is a best-case scenario assuming that regulatory activities resolve in our favor, negotiations go smoothly, and fundraising goals are met. But in projects such as this, the timeline cannot be certain. If, for example, Titan County approves Rupin's zoning request, Save Our River will appeal. This will delay activities to preserve the estate because it is unlikely that the family will settle on a purchase price without zoning resolution. Save Our River will inform the River Watch Foundation of delays and timeline adjustments.

TIMELINE: STOPPING DEVELOPMENT OF THE BURTON ESTATE

Tasks	Who is Responsible	When
1. Block Rupin's Rezoning Request to Titan County		
a. Develop brief on rezoning request	Save Our River (SOR) legal director	4/2015
b. Meet w/ County Planning Department	SOR exec. director & legal director	5/2015
c. Develop strategy to block rezoning	SOR; Swift Riverkeeper; Protect the Earth	5/2015
d. Begin implementing strategy	Board & staff of all allied organizations	5/2015
e. Begin developing/distributing information to media/supporters	SOR project director & communications director	6/2015
f. Testify at Commission rezoning hearing	Selected staff & board of SOR & allies	7/2015
g. Rupin's rezoning request denied	Titan County Commission	11/2015
2. Include Burton Wetlands in the Swift River System Wetlands Inventory		
a. Develop brief for U.S. Corps of Engineers & State Dept. of Natural Resources	SOR legal director & project director	5/2015
b. Meet with Corps of Engineers & Dept. of Natural Resources	SOR staff; Wildlife Guardians staff	6/2015
c. Develop strategy to include Burton wetlands in inventory	SOR staff; Wildlife Guardians staff	7/2015
d. Begin implementing strategy (includes seeking federal & state legislative support)	Board & staff of all allied organizations	7/2015
e. Estate wetlands included in inventory	Corps of Engineers; Dept. of Natural Resources	1/2016

Tasks	Who is Responsible	When
3. Amend Storm Water Regulations		
a. Develop proposed amendments	SOR legal director & project director	7/2015
b. Develop strategy to promote amendments	SOR staff; State Environmental Coalition	7/2015
c. Submit amendments to State Environmental Protection Agency	SOR exec. director	8/2015
d. Begin promoting amendments	Board & staff of all allied organizations	9/2015
e. Testify at storm water regulation hearings	Representatives of SOR & allied organizations	10/2015
f. Storm water regulations amended	State Environmental Protection Agency	2/2016

TIMELINE: LONG-TERM PRESERVATION OF THE BURTON ESTATE

1. Establish a State Park

a. Begin fundraising for estate's forested acres	Conserve Our Land (COL); SOR; allies	4/2015
b. Develop proposal and negotiating strategy for right of first refusal	SOR legal director, exec. director, project director; COL attorney	5/2015
c. Negotiate right of first refusal with Burton family	COL exec director, attorney; SOR exec. director, legal director	6/2015
d. Negotiate purchase with Burton family	COL exec. director, attorney; SOR exec. director, legal director	11/2015
e. Develop proposal to establish park	SOR exec. director & legal director	12/2015
f. Negotiate agreement w/ Dept. of Parks	COL exec. director, attorney; SOR exec. director, legal director	1/2016

Tasks	Who is Responsible	When
g. Complete fundraising	Board and staff of all allied organizations	3/2016
h. Purchase estate's forested land	COL	5/2016

2. Preserve Estate's Farmland

Tasks	Who is Responsible	When
a. Develop proposal for farm conservation easements	SOR legal director, project director; Farmsteads Unite	1/2016
b. Negotiate easements with Burton family, family attorney, State Dept. of Agriculture	SOR exec. director, legal director; Farmsteads Unite	2/2016
c. Begin to monitor & enforce easements	Farmsteads Unite	3/2016

CHECKLIST: METHODS

☐   1. Methods chosen respond to the causes of the problem.

☐   2. Methods chosen seem reasonable for producing proposed outcomes.

Methods Section:

☐   3. Starts with an overview.

☐   4. Includes justification of approach—explains why methods were selected.

☐   5. Describes who will benefit—the target population.

☐   6. Describes who will participate in funded activities, if different from target population.

☐   7. Describes major components of activity.

☐   8. Quantifies what the program will do—tells how much, how many, and by when.

☐   9. Describes staffing.

☐   10. Describes facilities, equipment, and supplies.

☐   11. Includes timeline or sequence of program activities.

☐   12. Provides a back-up plan if substantial barriers are anticipated.

☐   13. Aligns with budget.

If there will be collaboration:

☐   14. Describes plans for working with other organizations.

☐   15. Refers to documentation of collaboration located in appendix.

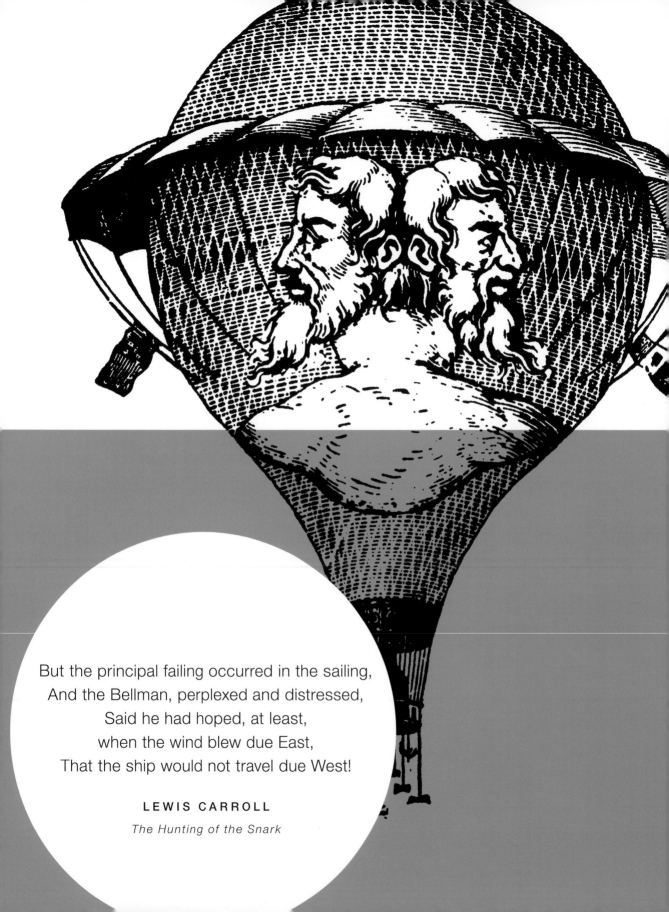

But the principal failing occurred in the sailing,
And the Bellman, perplexed and distressed,
Said he had hoped, at least,
when the wind blew due East,
That the ship would not travel due West!

LEWIS CARROLL
The Hunting of the Snark

Evaluation
How Will You Track Activities and Measure Results?

The Evaluation Section describes how your organization will assess whether the program is operating according to plan and achieving the intended outcomes.

Most funders require some kind of program evaluation. Even if they don't, there are plenty of reasons to make the effort.

Why Evaluate?

Effective programs. An objective evaluation can identify a program's strengths and weaknesses and guide program improvements. By weighing benefits against costs, an evaluation can also help save money. It's a tool of good management, saving an organization from squandering energy on activities that produce no results.

Broader knowledge base. An evaluation can identify particularly effective strategies—knowledge that can be useful when designing other programs. It can also focus attention on areas of concern—where more information may be needed. It can help other organizations avoid mistakes and provide yardsticks by which they can measure success.

Sustainable programs. Positive evaluation results are the surest proof that a program is succeeding. They show the quality of your work and can be key in securing support for the future.

Organizational credibility. Your organization can use positive evaluation results as the centerpiece of a public relations effort. Good results can also be used in grant proposals to show that your organization delivers what it promises. Even disappointing results can have value by demonstrating a commitment to self-examination and program improvement.

Evaluation may also be called

- evaluation plan
- program evaluation
- program assessment
- plan to measure
- measure of success

The Two Parts of an Evaluation

An evaluation plan has two distinct components: outcome evaluation and process evaluation. Each complements the other, and together, they give a full picture of a program's effectiveness.

The central and first task of evaluation is to assess whether the intended outcomes are being achieved, and how well. But you can't stop there. You also need to know why the program is succeeding or falling short. That's where process evaluation comes in. It looks at program implementation to determine why outcomes are or aren't happening.

Outcome Evaluation. This part of the evaluation measures results—how much change the program produces. Outcome evaluations typically examine:

- A program's effectiveness: To what degree is the program producing the expected outcomes? To what degree can changes be attributed to the program? What elements of the program are contributing to success or failure? Is the program cost-effective? Why or why not?

- A program's impact: Is the program contributing to longer-term outcomes? In what way? Have there been unintended outcomes, either positive or negative? What are they, and why did they happen?

- A program's continuing benefits: Can outcomes be sustained beyond the period of grant funding? If so, how can that be accomplished? If not, why?

Outcome Evaluation
may also be called

. . . .

summative evaluation
evaluation of program results
evaluation of accomplishments
impact evaluation

Process Evaluation
may also be called

. . . .

formative evaluation
evaluation of program
implementation

Process Evaluation. This part of the evaluation examines the methods used and whether the program is operating according to plan. It can help ensure that any change in strategy is intentional rather than accidental. Most important, it can help your organization decide which methods are most effective.

What if a program is wildly successful—achieving all expected outcomes—but it's not following the original plan? Or what if the program is not achieving the intended outcomes but has dutifully followed the original plan? No matter what, you have to look at how the program is operating to figure out whether the original plan is working or needs to be modified.

Process evaluations typically answer questions like these:

- How is the program being implemented?
- Is it proceeding as planned?
- Are there unexpected challenges?
- Are resources being used efficiently?
- Are changes in strategies required?

Designing the Evaluation

Before designing the evaluation, be sure your proposed program outcomes are clear, measurable, and achievable. If they're not, some rethinking and rewriting are needed. Evaluating a program's success or failure is nearly impossible if the proposed outcomes are vague or off target.

Then, consider: (1) what information your organization needs to prompt continuous improvement; (2) what funders will want to know; and (3) what will be meaningful to the larger community.

How complex must an evaluation be? That depends on the program design, the available resources, funder requirements, and the desire for in-depth findings vs. something less detailed. Planning and conducting rigorous scientific evaluations or evaluations of especially complex programs often require expert help. But a quality evaluation plan doesn't have to be complicated. It need only lay out an honest and objective system for assessing how well a program is working.

A good evaluation is

- an essential part of planning a program, and may begin before the program is launched
- right-sized—appropriate to the scope of the program
- systematic
- integrated with program activities.

Be realistic about your organization's ability to gather and analyze the data that will be the basis of the evaluation.

Don't make the plan so complicated that the staff can't carry it out. A simple, well-considered evaluation that can be accomplished is much better than an elaborate plan that never gets done.

Eight Essential Questions

Once you've determined what your organization needs to know, draft a set of questions. These primary questions are the framework of the evaluation plan. Make sure the questions align with the content of the Outcomes and Methods Sections.

The outcome evaluation and the process evaluation will provide different sorts of information. But each should address these eight items:

1. **What will be measured?** The *outcome* evaluation plan must tell the reader what you will measure to judge whether the program's predicted outcomes are being achieved.

   For example, a tutoring program may measure reading levels. A pollution abatement program may measure the amount of pesticide in the river. A substance abuse prevention program may measure youth attitudes that research has directly linked to drug use.

   The *process* evaluation plan will explain what you will measure to know if the program is proceeding as intended, and delivering the expected quantity of services within the proposed time frame.

   For example, a tutoring program may count the number of participants signed up within one month. A pollution abatement program may count the number of farmers who agree to pesticide-use audits within the first three months. A substance abuse prevention program may count the number of counseling groups held each week and the number of youth who participate voluntarily.

2. **What's the baseline?** It's not possible to gauge change without a starting point for measurement—a baseline.

   For example, in the *outcome* evaluation, the number of eighth graders reading below grade level can be the baseline for measuring the results of an expanded tutoring program. In the *process* evaluation, the number of children being tutored before the expanded program begins can be the baseline for measuring the success of student recruitment efforts.

Sometimes baseline data will not be available until the program begins. A program to reduce the body mass index of 25 obese diabetics must recruit its participants and take measurements to obtain baseline data. Be sure to collect baseline data as soon as possible. If a program gets rolling without it, the ability to accurately assess change will be compromised.

3. What information will be collected?

This will depend on what the program is trying to accomplish and the design of the evaluation.

In a tutoring program to increase the reading skills of children, the *outcome* evaluation may include collecting the results of reading tests, and the *process* evaluation may require logging children's participation in tutoring sessions.

If your organization is working to decrease pollution in a river, the *outcome* evaluation may require data collection of water samples, and the *process* evaluation may require detailed notes on staff interaction with local officials.

4. When will information be collected?

Evaluation is not a one-time event. It's an information-gathering strategy that runs throughout the life of a program and sometimes before and after. Data-collection schedules can vary. But *outcome* evaluation data are typically collected quarterly, upon completion of major components of the program, and at its finish. Data for *process* evaluation are often gathered continuously.

Major evaluation tasks such as contracting with an external evaluator, submitting evaluation reports, or conducting major surveys should be included in the program implementation timeline in the Methods Section. If the evaluation plan is especially complex, consider including a timeline here that lays out only the evaluation activities. If lots of different types of data will be gathered at different times from different groups of people using different instruments, such a timeline will make it easier for both your organization and funders to understand what will be happening when.

In rare instances, a funder may require that the evaluation measures the program's impact beyond the grant period. If so, be sure that adequate resources are budgeted and a system is put in place to satisfy such a demand.

5. How will information be collected?

When practical, use existing data sources. For example, the needed information may already be in your organization's database. Or perhaps public agency data such as school performance reports or health department statistics will work. When existing data sources can't provide what you need, you may have to gather *outcome* data by administering questionnaires, running focus groups, or taking physical measurements. The data you need for a *process* evaluation may come from attendance rosters, client intake forms, activity logs, feedback forms, minutes of meetings, newspaper clippings, correspondence, program reports, and such.

Designing an attendance roster or activity checklist is relatively simple. But designing more sophisticated evaluation tools such as questionnaires can be tricky.

Evaluation instruments that have stood up to heavy-duty scrutiny are called standardized, normed, reliable, and/or valid. Although these terms mean slightly different things, these instruments are likely to produce solid data when administered correctly. Use proven instruments when they're a good fit, rather than creating your own. They will carry more credibility than a tool your organization designs and will produce more dependable information.

When a proven tool doesn't quite work for a program, a bit of tinkering may make it usable. But when a proven tool is altered, it no longer qualifies as standardized, normed, reliable, and/or valid, and that could be a problem if the funder requires professional quality data. If your organization lacks the expertise to modify a proven tool, consider asking an outside expert to help.

If your organization decides to design its own evaluation tools, be aware of the risks. Poorly constructed tools can result in data that are tainted, difficult to manage, incomplete, confusing, or even worthless.

6. **Who will collect the information?** When information is objective—for example, a test score, a statistic from the health department—the expertise and objectivity of the person collecting it is seldom an issue. But if data sources are subjective or data collection requires special expertise, then it matters who collects the data.

For example, getting objective data from a focus group requires skill and impartiality. The manner in which a survey is administered can affect its results. The competence of the person taking blood pressure readings affects accuracy.

Be sure the evaluation plan identifies who will collect the data and, if relevant, cites the credentials or experience that qualifies them.

7. **How will data be analyzed?** Having described what data will be collected, the Evaluation Section must explain how it will be deciphered. For example, you may propose a trend analysis, comparing local data to national norms, or you may assess the relationship between costs and program outcomes.

Sometimes staff members gather data that are later analyzed by an evaluation expert. Sometimes a contracted evaluator does both data gathering and analysis. Be sure to identify the people who will analyze the data and what qualifies them to do so.

8. **What reports will be produced when, and how will they be used?** Evaluation reports can be issued quarterly, every six months, or at some other interval. No matter the timing, set up a regular reporting schedule, even if the funder doesn't require it. Informative reports issued on a timely basis provide a dependable stream of information to help your organization make sound program decisions.

Because evaluation reports distill data and summarize conclusions, they provide vital feedback that you can use to improve a program. They also keep the funder informed, let the community know what's being learned, and are a way to share findings with others in the field. By discussing accomplishments and challenges, evaluation reports demonstrate that your organization is accountable and committed to continuous improvement.

COST BENEFIT & COST-EFFECTIVENESS?

Cost-benefit analysis is an attempt to relate the costs of a program to its social benefits. Cost-effectiveness assumes that of two programs which have approximately the same social benefit, the one that costs less is more cost-effective.

Say that a community-based program offering an alternative to imprisonment has an offender recidivism rate comparable to that of a state prison. If the cost per offender is lower at the community program, the social benefits of the two options are the same but the community alternative is more cost-effective.

Considering costs and benefits can often tell you whether the program is worth the price tag. And when relevant, a discussion of cost benefit or cost-effectiveness can be a powerful argument for funding.

Include Hard & Soft Data

Hard data are quantitative information that can be tallied, or measured. Soft data are qualitative information that reflects the personal experiences of program participants and beneficiaries. Each serves a particular purpose. Hard data are objective but can be awfully dry. Soft data are subjective, but on their own can make funders wonder if there are numbers to support them. Your organization needs to collect both hard and soft data to get the full story and properly evaluate the impact of a program.

For a program to reduce pollution in a lake, hard data for the *outcome* evaluation might be the level of phosphates in the lake or the concentration of algae. Hard data for the *process* evaluation could be the number of people attending informational meetings or the number of farmers agreeing to reduce fertilizer-contaminated runoff.

Soft data are typically gathered through observation, interviews, open-ended survey questions, and a review of written material. They may be anecdotal. They can reveal why methods do or don't work, and how the community views the program. Soft data can also give expression to results that are hard to quantify—tears of joy, pride in accomplishment, hope.

Consider the example of the program to reduce lake pollution. Soft data for the *outcome* evaluation might come from the comments of local physicians who treat swimmers for ear infections and skin rashes. They might also come from newspaper stories that shed light on community opinion about the lake's condition. Soft data for the *process* evaluation could be gathered by reviewing transcripts of community meetings to better understand community concerns. Or interviewers could ask farmers what influenced their decisions about managing runoff.

Who Will Conduct the Evaluation?

The evaluation can be planned and conducted by your staff or outside evaluation experts (often called third-party evaluators) or a combination of both. Here are the trade-offs.

Independent Evaluation Experts. Qualified consultants can contribute perspectives and skills beyond an organization's in-house capabilities. Their résumés and arm's-length objectivity can also give funders confidence that the evaluation will be professional and unbiased. Consultants can help articulate measurable program outcomes and write the evaluation section of the grant proposal.

But buyer beware. Without a thorough understanding of your organization, an outsider may propose a plan that's unrealistic, insensitive to constituents, or useless. When vetting a potential evaluator, conduct an in-depth interview, interview past clients, and review examples of prior work if possible. Make sure the consultant is knowledgeable in your organization's field of interest and would be a good fit with the staff.

When deciding whether to use an outside evaluator, consider these questions:

- Is the evaluator well qualified?

- Is the evaluator a good match for your organization and for the specific program?

- Can the evaluator participate in developing the proposal? Because funders rarely cover expenses before a grant is awarded, your organization will have to pick up the tab or ask the consultant to consider this preliminary work as an investment.

- What will the evaluation cost? Can the cost be covered by the grant? If not, where will the money come from?

When you need an evaluation expert, you'll often need one quickly. Here are a few ideas for beginning your search:

- Funders that require evaluation are likely to know evaluators they can recommend.

- University faculty members often have training and experience in evaluation. Some do consulting or can recommend qualified graduate students.

- Colleague organizations may have suggestions.

- State agencies that administer grants may recommend experts in your organization's area of interest.

- Private research firms, even those that don't specialize in your organization's field, often have professional contacts that might be useful in your search.

Finally, when you've hired an outside expert, be vigilant. You must maintain close oversight to make sure your organization gets what it needs.

In-House Evaluation. Using your organization's staff to run the evaluation will cost less than bringing in outside consultants. Staff members will also know more about your organization, the target population, and what the program is trying to accomplish. But on the downside, staff may not have the knowledge or experience to design a solid plan, and operating the evaluation may infringe on other work. Most important, even a well-designed in-house evaluation may appear to be or actually be biased.

When deciding whether to assign the task to your organization's staff, consider these questions:

- Does anyone on staff have the expertise to do it?

- Will evaluation responsibilities detract from staff's ability to perform other essential tasks?

- Can an in-house evaluation be objective?

- What will it cost?

If the decision is to handle the evaluation in-house, here are a few sources you can turn to for advice on the evaluation approach and available evaluation instruments:

- Talk to colleagues in other organizations that have evaluated similar programs. They may be able to offer tips, evaluation tools, and even copies of evaluation plans you could review and revise as needed.

- Post questions to online professional groups that focus on your organization's field of interest.

- Contact the state or national associations in your organization's area of interest and explore available resources, tools, and training.

- Contact state or national associations that focus on evaluation.

- Do some research on the Internet, or look for relevant publications.

- Engage an expert to help identify evaluation tools that would be appropriate.

When Funders Evaluate. Some funders conduct their own evaluations. In such cases, your organization must agree to participate even if the evaluation has yet to be designed. Federal agencies, for example, sometimes solicit proposals for evaluation services at the same time that they solicit proposals for the programs that will be evaluated. As a part of their evaluation, funders could require that your organization submit specific information to a database or complete questionnaires. They could also make site visits, examine files, and interview staff and clients.

A funder's evaluation may not generate all the information your organization wants. For that reason, it's wise to include a simple evaluation plan of your own in the program design. If the funder's final design works for your organization, you can merge efforts once the program is under way.

No Money for Evaluation? Do It Anyway

Even if grant funds won't cover the cost of an expert evaluator and staff time is limited, plan to conduct an evaluation. Identify the most critical questions and the data that are needed to answer them, and integrate data collection, analysis, and reporting into the program's ongoing activities. A minimal evaluation is better than none at all.

When there's no money for evaluation and you're on a tight deadline for submitting a funding proposal, you may be tempted to treat the evaluation plan as an afterthought. But don't. Take it seriously and by all means avoid pitfalls such as the following:

Mentioning some nebulous process.
"Evaluation will be conducted by:

(1) a weekly conference of the multidisciplinary team; and

(2) maintenance of comprehensive records and explicit documentation."

Saying an expert will take care of it later.
"To assure the success of this project, Dr. Jones of the University of Faraway will be employed to design an evaluation of the program."

Taking brevity to an absurd degree.
"The evaluation will consist of ongoing review of data derived from the survey, and examination of information obtained at the initial interview so that program outcomes can be tracked."

Ethics & Confidentiality

The data in evaluation reports can identify program participants, damage their reputations, or worse. Your organization has an obligation to assess the risks that an evaluation presents and to respond appropriately. Each participant should be told up front what the evaluation will entail. In addition, participants are commonly informed that:

- they can refuse to take part in the evaluation or refuse to answer specific questions

- they can opt out of the evaluation at any time

- they have a right to receive the benefits of the program even if they decline to participate in the evaluation

- their personal information will remain confidential.

Evaluation results are often presented in the aggregate, and reports carefully mask the identities of individuals. In such cases, participants usually are not asked for consent.

Some evaluations operate under the rules of implied consent, meaning that once participants are informed of the process, their consent is assumed unless they state otherwise.

However, some situations—and some funders—require that participants sign informed consent statements. The statement affirms they are willing to participate and verifies that they understand their rights and what the evaluation involves. If you're not certain which procedure to follow, seek expert advice.

When the evaluation collects data about individuals, your organization must ensure the data remain confidential and may not disclose the data without written permission. Documents containing names and other personal information must be handled carefully and stored securely. Some evaluators assign unique codes to protect participants' identities while allowing continued tracking of their progress.

The Health Insurance Portability and Accountability Act of 1996 (HIPAA) imposes specific, stringent confidentiality requirements for organizations that collect health (including mental health) data. If your organization is in this category, it must educate staff about the law and be sure evaluation plans meet HIPAA requirements.

Even when it is not a legal requirement, confidentiality is an ethical obligation.

Sensitivity to Participants

The evaluation plan must be appropriate for the people involved in the program. Instruments must be geared to the correct developmental stages of children or reading levels of adults. They must be suitable for the culture of participants and produced in their language. Focus groups and interviews must be conducted with sensitivity to the culture and circumstances of those being evaluated.

One of the best ways to ensure sensitivity is to involve the target population in planning the evaluation and selecting the tools.

EXAMPLES: EVALUATION

The first two examples are charts showing how to organize an evaluation plan. The first is an outcome evaluation; the second is a process evaluation. Charts such as these can make planning an evaluation more manageable and, in some situations, may be all that's needed for the grant proposal.

EXAMPLE 1: Organizing an Outcome Evaluation for Let's Read Together

This example lays out a plan for evaluating an outcome expected to result from a two-year reading program. In the first year, students will receive tutoring for six months, between January and June 2015. Evaluation data will be analyzed and reported by September 2015. Because an interim report will be available within eight months of program start-up, staff can use evaluation findings to prepare for the second year of the program.

Outcome 1: Within 6 months of program start-up, 16 of 20 ninth graders (80%) who now read at seventh-grade level will advance their reading skills by one grade level.

Evaluation Questions	**Question 1:** How many students improved their reading skills during this period, & how many did not? **Question 2:** Of those who improved, how much did each improve? **Question 3:** What do children who improved their reading skills have in common? What do children who did not improve their reading skills have in common?
Data Sources	**Questions 1 & 2:** Data provided by school from standardized reading test scores: • Baseline data from December 2014 test • Comparative data from June 2015 test **Question 3:** • Student Reading Skill Checklist[1] completed by students • Tutor/Student Match Rating Scale[2] completed by tutors & students
How Data Will Be Collected & By Whom	**Questions 1 & 2:** Special educator, Sal Jacobs, will collect data and prepare spreadsheets for analysis. **Question 3:** Tara Flynn, evaluation consultant, will administer the Student Reading Skill Checklist & the Tutor/Student Match Rating Scale and tabulate results.
When Data Will Be Collected, Analyzed, & Reported	School will provide baseline data by January 2015. June 2015 standardized reading test results will be collected by July 31, 2015. Student Reading Skill Checklist and Tutor/Student Match Rating Scale results will be tabulated by July 15, 2015. Data analysis and evaluation will be completed by Tara Flynn by August 15, 2015. Tara Flynn will submit interim evaluation report to program coordinator, principal, and school board by September 5, 2015.

[1] Standardized scale to assess factors affecting a student's reading skills.
[2] Standardized scale by Tutor Techniques, Inc., to assess efficacy of tutor/student match.

EXAMPLE 2: Organizing a Process Evaluation for Let's Read Together

This example is based on the same tutoring program as Example 1. It uses one activity—volunteer recruitment—to demonstrate the organization of a process evaluation. Individual charts such as the following can be created for each major activity component when planning a process evaluation.

Program Activity	Documentation of Accomplishment	How Data Will Be Collected & By Whom	When Data Will Be Collected
Recruit qualified volunteer tutors	• 2 newspaper ads • Meeting agendas of local organizations showing 3 recruitment presentations • E-mails to 4 local churches & 2 area universities • Letters to 10 community organizations	Program coordinator will collect copies of all recruitment documentation.	During the 2 months of volunteer recruitment

Program Activity	Documentation of Accomplishment	How Data Will Be Collected & By Whom	When Data Will Be Collected
Enlist 20 qualified volunteer tutors	• Results of background check in each volunteer file • Coordinator notes on screening interviews • Résumés of tutors on file • 20 signed volunteer agreements	Program coordinator will maintain a file on each volunteer and tabulate data on volunteer credentials.	During the 30 days of volunteer enlistment

EXAMPLE 3: Dads Work Program

The *Dads Work Program* is a new three-year program sponsored by the local Community Action Agency. It targets 25 noncustodial fathers who are not in compliance with court-ordered child-support payments. The fathers will be either unemployed or employed in low-paying jobs. The program is intended to help participants increase their earnings so that they can make regular child-support payments. It will provide intense assistance for one year, plus follow-up contact and monitoring for an additional two years.

EVALUATION PLAN

Dr. Ashim Nagi, Assistant Director of the Center for Evaluation (see attached résumé), designed the Dads Work *evaluation plan and will serve as the program's third-party evaluator.*

Process Evaluation

The process evaluation will use data from an electronic journal and from structured interviews with participants.

The program director will maintain a weekly electronic journal answering questions designed by Dr. Nagi. (See attached questions.) Entries will address: (1) conformance with timeline; (2) quantity of service delivered (i.e., number of fathers participating and the hours of instruction and counseling provided to each); (3) problems encountered; (4) solutions and successes; and (5) adjustments to program design.

Dr. Nagi will interview each father three times: upon entry and at the sixth and twelfth months of the program. Using a structured interview format, Dr. Nagi will talk with each father about his: (1) self-assessment of progress; (2) challenges in meeting program requirements; (3) motivations for continued participation; (4) satisfaction with the program; and (5) suggestions for program improvement.

Dr. Nagi will prepare quarterly reports assessing program implementation and lessons learned. The program director and executive director will use the reports to refine approaches and inform funders of progress.

Outcome Evaluation

Baseline data will be gathered when each father enters the program. Counselors will complete a weekly report on each participant's progress. (See attached progress report form.)

Outcome #1: Within one year of entering the program, 20 of 25 fathers (80%) will increase their earnings to a level that enables them to make required child-support payments.

The income needed by each participant will be calculated when he enters the program. To increase his income to an adequate level, a participant must do one of the following:

- *get a job that pays the required salary*
- *become certified in a trade in which the average earnings meet the necessary income criteria*
- *get a promotion that increases income to the needed level.*

Fathers will document their income by providing counselors with proof of employment and salary level, copy of trade certification, or proof of promotion and salary increase.

Counselors will note each father's progress in a weekly report. Examples of progress indicators include:

- *increased employment skills*
- *completion of classes related to employment*
- *acceptance into a trade certification program*

- *identification of jobs at the required pay level for which the father is qualified*
- *applications submitted for jobs at or above desired salary level*
- *interviews obtained for jobs that pay the required salary.*

Outcome #2: *Within one year of entering the program, 20 of 25 fathers (80%) will make required child-support payments on time.*

With participants' permission, program counselors will collaborate with the state Child Support Agency to track each father's compliance for the three years of his participation in the program. (See attached letter from Child Support Agency.)

Counselors will note each father's progress in weekly reports. Examples of progress indicators include:

- *fewer missed monthly payments*
- *increased number of full, rather than partial, payments*
- *increased number of on-time payments*
- *payroll deduction plan to make payments.*

Counselors will complete quarterly assessments that will be summarized by Dr. Nagi in quarterly progress reports. Dr. Nagi will combine both process and outcome evaluation data to identify which materials and services are most effective.

Annual Evaluation Report

Sixty days after the end of each program year, Dr. Nagi will submit an annual report addressing the following questions:

1. *Was the program implemented as planned?*
2. *Were there deviations from the original program design? If so, why?*
3. *What challenges affected program implementation? How were they addressed?*
4. *To what degree is the program achieving its proposed outcomes?*
5. *What services and materials are most effective in producing the outcomes?*
6. *Were there unexpected outcomes, positive or negative?*

The program director and executive director will present the report to the board of directors and discuss findings with the funder.

Confidentiality

When entering the program, each father will receive a written overview of the evaluation plan. A counselor will explain the plan, as well as the father's right to decline participation and yet still receive services. The father will sign an informed consent form to document his choice. The form will also document the father's understanding that if he chooses to take part, he may still refuse to answer certain questions and may opt out of the evaluation entirely at any time.

All data will be stored in the agency's central database, which is maintained on a secure network server and protected with appropriate firewalls and passwords. Hard copies of participant records and program data will be stored in locked filing cabinets. Access to client data will be limited to the evaluation consultant, program director, administrative assistant, and executive director.

EXAMPLE 4: Eighth Grade Get Fit Program

A community organization and a middle school are partners in a program to improve the physical fitness of students. The evaluation will be guided by an experienced evaluator.

Evaluation Plan

Sung Kim, Program Coordinator, who has conducted three other evaluations for the Child Health Organization (the Organization), will lead this evaluation. Both the Organization and City Middle School are experienced in data collection and adhere to strict participant-protection protocols.

Ms. Kim will gather and analyze data regularly, as described in the chart below. She will meet with staff quarterly to review data and to plan program improvements.

Teachers will assess the physical fitness of participating students during the first week of the program and then quarterly, using resting heart rate and body mass index measurements. Students will take the Lets Move It Survey (attached) during the first week of the program (pre-test) and again at the end of the program (post-test) to document their activity levels and attitudes regarding fitness and exercise. Together, these data will document how changes in activity levels and attitudes contribute to the program outcomes.

This evaluation plan has been approved by the Organization, the school, and the Parent Teacher Association. The letter sent to parents describing the program will also inform them that their child's participation in the evaluation is not required.

Evaluation documents will be stored in locked file cabinets, and electronic files will be password protected. Access to evaluation files will be managed by Ms. Kim.

The chart below details the outcome and process evaluation plan.

Outcome Evaluation Question	How Question Will Be Answered
Are participating students: a. improving physical fitness? or b. maintaining the optimum recommended level of physical fitness?	• Quarterly analysis of fitness data (resting heart rates and body mass indexes) gathered by the school's physical education teachers

Process Evaluation Question	How Question Will Be Answered
1. Did 150 of the school's 200 8th graders (75%) hit the targeted 180 minutes/week of moderate physical activity through the *Get Fit Program*?	• Quarterly review of student participation logs in *Get Fit Program* activities • Analysis of pre/post Let's Move It Survey results
2. Did 150 of the school's 200 8th graders (75%) enjoy *Get Fit Program* activities?	• Analysis of pre/post Let's Move It Survey results

Ms. Kim will submit a quarterly report to the organization's executive director and the school's principal. The report will be used to monitor program implementation; assess program outcomes; determine if a change in approach is warranted; and update the Parent Teacher Association, school board, and funder. Ms. Kim will submit an annual report two months after the end of the program.

A FEW DEFINITIONS

Baseline data: Data that provide a starting point from which change is then measured.

Data: Information of all sorts including facts, figures, statistics, responses to interview questions, test results, quotes, and more.

Evaluation instrument or tool: Survey, test, questionnaire, or other device used to collect data.

Indicators: The data used to document program implementation and to measure change.

Reliable instrument: A survey, test, or questionnaire proven to produce consistent results in evaluations, experiments, or clinical trials.

Pre/Post test: An instrument administered to the target population before beginning a program and again at the end of the program. It allows change to be measured by comparing the pre-program and post-program test results.

Standardized or normed instrument: An evaluation tool that has been tested with a large number of people in a specific population in order to define "normal" scores for that population. A certain range of scores is considered normal, and scores outside that range are considered abnormal.

Third-party evaluator: An evaluation expert who is not directly affiliated with the organization being evaluated.

Valid instrument: A survey, test, or questionnaire that has been rigorously examined and has been proven to measure what it is designed to measure.

CHECKLIST: EVALUATION

☐   1. Presents complementary plans for evaluating outcomes and methods.

☐   2. Identifies who will conduct the evaluation and describes evaluator's qualifications.

☐   3. Answers "a" through "g" below for both outcome and process evaluation.

OUTCOME	PROCESS	
☐	☐	a. What primary questions will the evaluation address?
☐	☐	b. What will be measured?
☐	☐	c. What is the baseline, or starting point?
☐	☐	d. What information will be collected and when?
☐	☐	e. Will hard (quantitative) and soft (qualitative) data be collected?
☐	☐	f. How will information be collected and by whom?
☐	☐	g. How will the information be analyzed?

☐   4. Describes the approach for keeping data confidential, when applicable.

☐   5. Is culturally appropriate for participants.

☐   6. Indicates what reports will be produced.

☐   7. Describes how the reports will be used.

☐   8. Describes how evaluation results will contribute to improving the program.

Then the grasshopper
knew it is best
to prepare for the
days of necessity.

AESOP

The Ant and the Grasshopper

Future Support
Sustaining Impact After the Grant

This is the last section of the narrative portion of your proposal, but by no means the least. Funders want to know that their grant awards are good investments that will yield long-term social benefits. This section is where you show you are planning to sustain the program's impact.

Grant funding is sometimes called *soft money* because it usually lasts only one to five years. Some funders renew grants for longer periods, but few want to adopt a program as a long-term dependent. If a program will accomplish its aims within the grant period, this is not a concern. But if beneficiaries will still need the program after the grant ends, there has to be a plan for future support.

When a program changes the way a system operates (strengthens antipollution laws, makes access to higher education more equitable, etc.) achieving the intended outcomes promises ongoing results. If your program will produce enduring benefits without the need for maintaining program activities, explain why.

But often, sustaining impact means that the program, or some portion of it, needs to continue to operate. In that case, planning for the future can't wait until the last minute. It must be an integral part of initial planning.

The program you maintain beyond grant funding may look quite different than the original. You'll drop activities that aren't producing results; parts of the program may be adopted into other organizations; and available resources may mean some program components get scaled down.

Remember, program activities are only a means to an end, and that end is results. It's not important that the program continue exactly as it began. But it is important that lessons learned are used to carry positive change into the future.

Focusing on sustained results will influence many program planning decisions, guiding you to target root causes of the problem, to build authentic collaborations, and to embed the work deeply into the community.

It will also influence budget development, prompting questions such as: Is it more important to be centrally located or to keep costs down by working in a donated, but more remote space? Is it more cost-effective to train volunteers in-person with an expert or to save money by using a computerized training system?

The key point is that when planning a program and then developing a grant proposal, your organization must keep the future in mind. Plan for the long run, so that the investment of grant funds is more likely to yield enduring benefits.

The more specific the plan, the more it will instill confidence. Don't say something vague like *"To continue our program beyond the period of the federal grant, we'll seek support from local governments, foundations, businesses, and any other sources that offer funding for which we may qualify."*

Future Support
May also be called

- Sustaining Impact
- Sustainability
- Future Funding
- Plan for Program Continuation

Four Essential Elements

Funders realize that a gilt-edged guarantee of sustainability is unlikely, but they expect the proposal to show there's a plan for the future. When explaining how you'll tackle sustainability, be sure to address these four essential elements.

1. A Leader. Staff in most nonprofits work at maximum capacity. If sustaining effective activities isn't in the job description, that work will get pushed to the back of the to-do list. Designate a person to take on sustainability as a regular task.

2. Data. To know which activities are producing results, you've got to have data. And data will help rally the community to keep successful activities going. Be sure the evaluation plan connects activities to outcomes and produces the information you need to engage others. Explain how evaluation data will inform and support your work to continue positive results.

3. Community Support. When planning and operating programs, engage organizations with intersecting missions. Build an active community advisory council that includes partner organizations, beneficiaries, volunteers, and community leaders. Be sure your proposal shows how this important web of support will be established and maintained. Genuine and vigorous community support can inspire creative ideas for sustaining impact beyond fundraising.

4. A Plan. If you've got a preliminary plan in place, explain it. If you'll hammer out a plan later, after assessing evaluation results, explain that. Describe how you'll involve the community advisory council and spell out questions you'll ask as part of the planning process. For example, how will you determine which activities to continue? What resources will you explore and what approaches will you consider? Tell the reader how the overall plan will roll out.

Ideas for Future Support
Can Your Organization Fund It?

If your organization is robust enough, it may be able to fund successful program activities. Even when money is tight, it may be able to allocate or reallocate funds to support approaches that are an especially good fit.

For example, a school might fund a tutoring program that is improving academic performance. A hospital might fund a hand-washing program that is decreasing patient infections.

If this is your plan, include a letter of commitment from the board of directors. If a commitment would be premature, document that your organization will consider a commitment when it has seen enough data from the evaluation.

If your organization can show that it has assumed the costs of other programs previously funded by grants, that will boost credibility of the plan.

Turn It Over to Another Organization

Your organization's success with a project may convince another organization with similar interests to adopt it and keep it going. For example, a program to repair hiking trails might be taken over by the state forest service. A youth theater troupe might be adopted by a large performing arts center. If this is the plan, provide evidence of collaboration with the organization that you hope will adopt the program, and document that the organization will consider assuming responsibility.

Begin or Expand Fund Development

A fund development program is a systematic effort to establish and nurture diverse, reliable funding streams. It reaches beyond the soft money an organization may raise from grants. Fund development programs bring in hard money from sources such as committed donors that, with diligent stewardship, can be renewed regularly and increased over time.

If fund development revenue will be part of your plan to continue successful activities, include a letter of commitment from the board of directors. Specify how much money directors expect to raise and where it will come from.

Here are examples of fund development strategies:

Membership fees. Individuals, companies, and other organizations pay a fee to join your organization. In addition to the satisfaction of supporting activities they care about, members receive benefits such as newsletters, discounts, and special admission to performances.

Annual fund appeals. An organization uses mailers, e-mails, and telephone calls to make a broad appeal for annual contributions.

Major gifts. Staff and board members identify individuals who are committed to your organization or its cause and who have the financial means to provide substantial donations. Then board members and other volunteers reach out to prospects and encourage contributions. The goal is to establish loyal relationships that lead to gifts ranging from thousands to millions of dollars.

Planned gifts. These are estate-planning tools which can benefit both the donor and a non-profit organization. They require the expertise of lawyers, certified public accountants, or other specialists. The gifts are often deferred and may serve a variety of purposes for the donor, including tax advantages. Planned-giving includes bequests, charitable lead and remainder trusts, pooled life income funds, annuities, life insurance, and retained life interest in donated personal property or real estate.

Endowment. Think of this as your organization's savings account. Money is permanently set aside and invested, the principal goes untouched, but earned interest may be spent as your organization sees fit. An endowment is an approach for establishing a permanent source of predictable income.

Special events. Walkathons, auctions, holiday galas, and other events raise awareness about your cause, engage volunteers, and are often the first point of contact with future donors. Organizations nurture such contacts in hopes that newcomers will become members, regular contributors, and eventually major donors. Events can generate large sums of money.

Begin or Expand Earned Income

Your organization may already use some earned income approaches, but there could be other excellent possibilities waiting to be discovered. The best earned income strategies will both reinforce an organization's mission and produce additional funds. Charging for something your organization already does or renting unused space are common ways to bring in extra money. Here are examples of earned income strategies:

Merchandise. Many organizations sell things to raise money—cookies, cookbooks, clothing, publications, and so forth. This is a flexible and expandable source of income.

Client fees. Your organization may be able to charge a fee for services. A sliding-fee scale based on ability to pay will provide income while still keeping services accessible to those who need them.

If you plan to use this strategy, briefly describe the income levels of clients and how the sliding-fee scale will be constructed. Be sure to note the fees customarily charged for such services. Estimate the volume of services your organization will provide at each fee level to calculate expected income. Begin charging fees early in the life of the program so this income stream will be in place when the grant ends.

Third-party payments. When the cost of a service is paid by a source other than those who receive it or those who deliver it, that's called a third-party payment. The cost of your organization's services might be eligible for third-party reimbursement from insurance companies or government subsidy programs.

If your organization has an established system for receiving third-party payments, describe it and the revenue it is expected to generate. If there's no system in place, describe how your organization's program will qualify for such payments, the steps you will take to establish a system, and the expected revenue.

A business. When planning a business, be sure there's a market for the products or services, that the business is a fit with your organization's mission, and that nonprofit status won't be jeopardized. Because of the possible ramifications for your organization's nonprofit status, it's best to get the advice of an expert.

If you propose a business venture, the funder will want to know something about the business plan, why you think the venture will succeed, and what profit you expect.

Explore Federated Fundraising

When a charity such as United Way conducts a fundraising drive and distributes the proceeds to organizations it has accepted as members, that's called *federated fundraising*. If such cooperative efforts exist locally, explore them. If your organization proposes this strategy, describe the application process, the likelihood of acceptance, and how much money it might bring in.

Investigate Public Funding

Local, regional, and state governments sometimes support projects with general funds, tax and bond levies, or user fees. If you propose this strategy, describe the expected time-frame for funding and why you believe your organization will receive the funds it requests. The plan will be more convincing if your organization has a track record of public funding.

Grant Hopping

Replacing one short-term grant with another can buy time while your organization searches for longer-term funding streams. But until long-term sources are in place, the future of the program is not secure. *Hopping from grant to grant is not a solid strategy.*

Applying for a grant is a gamble. There is no guarantee of success, even for a high-quality proposal for a well-planned program. Your proposal may be passed over for any number of reasons unrelated to merit. The funder might want a broader geographic distribution of awards and may have already funded programs in your area. It might want to support a different target population than the one you propose. Or another applicant may have established a track record with the funder or enjoy a special connection.

Funders have different interests, and many won't be a good match for a specific program. Be selective and be aware that some funding opportunities can lure you off course. If your plan to continue the program is to just get another grant—any grant—you'll be tempted to reshape the program just to get the money. Focusing on funding rather than the real purpose of the program can ruin the program.

Documenting Commitments

If your organization is fortunate enough to have commitments for future funding in place, tell where that support will come from and include documentation in the appendix. Even if the commitment is pending, your proposal will be significantly strengthened by the possibility.

For example, a plan that relies in part on expanding an annual fund appeal will be fortified by a letter from your organization's board pledging to raise more money. If the school may adopt your organization's tutoring program, include a letter from the school board expressing their intent to seriously consider that possibility.

Commitment of Leadership

Before applying for a grant, your organization's board of directors and administrators must consider the implications of starting a new program. How does it fit with the strategic plan? If the program must be continued beyond grant funding, how will that affect the organization? Directors will need to weigh benefits to clients against future financial obligations and then decide whether to move forward.

The commitment of the organization's leaders is a major factor. If they're sold on a program and willing to accept its long-term financial demands, their enthusiasm can help it survive after the grant ends.

Leadership's commitment to evaluation is also important, because evaluation shows whether the program is producing benefits. If it is, the organization will have the facts needed to seek ongoing funding or bring on partners. If it's not, the organization will know that it must make changes in the program. If the verdict is that the program is not worth continuing—that it was a good try that didn't work—it's a valuable lesson learned.

Good Habits

There are organizational habits that can play an important role in continuing grant-funded programs:

Spread the word. Help sometimes comes from unexpected sources. Informing the public about programs can be a great investment. Good public relations often pay off in surprising ways.

Involve others. A program that includes volunteers, businesses, partner

Involve others. A program that includes volunteers, businesses, partner organizations, and others is better positioned to endure than one that's operated in isolation. People and groups that care about a program will voice support, contribute resources, and help make beneficial connections.

Connect with community leaders. In every community there are people, whether they have prestigious titles or not, who make things happen. Find out who they are and introduce them to your organization's work.

Develop relationships with funders. Money is just one thing they have to offer. Funders can also provide ideas, advice, and

EXAMPLE: FUTURE SUPPORT

The City Health Clinic is seeking a two-year start-up grant from the Children's Foundation for a program that will help both children with chronic serious illness and their parents. The children, usually isolated at home or in the hospital, will enjoy time with other children and receive health care in a welcoming environment. Parents will receive counseling and respite from the demands of caring for a seriously ill child. This program is expected to improve the mental health of the children and their parents, and to increase family stability.

The Clinic's proposal for start-up funds includes the following plan for continuing the new program beyond the two-year grant period. The plan includes new financial and in-kind resources, shows that organizers have already made extensive contacts, and offers evidence of broad community commitment. All of this greatly enhances the plan's credibility in this good example.

Our House Respite Program

If the program evaluation demonstrates that the Our House Respite Program is effective, our organization will establish a system to support it indefinitely. Because we are confident that the program will be successful, we are already working to develop ongoing support through three approaches.

1. Fee-for-service

(A) Sliding fee scale: The State Department of Health will help us develop a sliding fee scale for service. (See letter in appendix.) The scale will be based on income level and will be applied when costs cannot be recovered from health

insurance, Medicaid, or government subsidy programs. Based on fees charged in other locations for similar services to similar clients, our conservative estimate is that this income stream will support 2% of the budget by year two, and 3% in year three and onward. No family will be denied service because of their inability to make payment toward costs.

(B) Third-party payments: Similar programs in other locations serving similar clients secure between 50% and 60% of their funding from insurance payments and government subsidies. There are four insurance companies in our area that reimburse for the services we will provide. (See attached list.) Our financial manager and clinical director will work with each insurance company and with the State Department of Health to establish a system similar to those used by other organizations for such reimbursements. Preliminary discussions indicate that it will take approximately two years to establish this funding stream. Our plan assumes that we will receive 40% of program funding from this source by year three of operation and just over 56% by year four. (See attached letters documenting discussions.)

2. Resources from partner organizations

(A) The State University Hospital has made a five-year commitment to provide 500 square feet of space and 17 hours per week of nursing assistance. The space is valued at $10 per square foot per month amounting to an annual in-kind contribution of $60,000. Nursing assistance, valued at $32.94 per hour (salary and benefits) amounts to a cash contribution of $29,120 in the first year. In each subsequent year, the budget includes a 4% salary increase. The board of the hospital will consider continuing this commitment beyond the initial five years if the program proves successful. (See attached letter of commitment.)

(B) The Family Service Center has agreed to provide 16 hours per week of counseling service for four years and to consider continuing this service if the program proves successful. A counselor's time, valued at $31.25 per hour (salary and benefits) amounts to a cash contribution of $26,000 in the first year. In each subsequent year, the budget includes a 4% salary increase. (See attached letter of commitment.)

3. Partnerships with local charities

(A) The Parents Wellness Association has pledged to raise $15,000 to cover funding shortfalls in year three. This group has a successful track record of raising funds for similar programs, and its pledge is evidence of strong community support. (See attached letter of commitment.)

(B) The United Way has agreed to consider making a nonmember grant of $29,131. We will apply for the grant in year two and use it to support year three, during which our third-party payment system will still be maturing. Because program costs are expected to escalate at 4% per year, we will apply for membership in United Way in year four and use its expected $50,000 annual allocation in year five and onward to sustain our initial level of service and establish an operating reserve if possible. (See attached letter of support and interest from United Way.)

The following chart shows our plan for sustaining Our House Respite Program beyond the two-year grant period:

Funding Source	Year 1	Year 2	Year 3	Year 4
Children's Foundation Grant Request	150,000	152,895		
Fee for Service		5,505	8,605	8,948
Third-Party Payments			114,410	167,283
State University Hospital	89,120	90,285	91,496	92,756
Family Service Center	26,000	27,040	28,122	29,247
Parents Wellness Association			15,000	
United Way Nonmember Grant			29,131	
TOTAL	**265,120**	**275,725**	**286,764**	**298,234**

CHECKLIST: FUTURE SUPPORT

☐   1. Describes specific, realistic, and credible approaches for sustaining the impact of the program after the grant ends.

☐   2. When appropriate, briefly cites track record with similar approaches.

☐   3. Provides a detailed description of support that is already committed.

☐   4. Includes documentation of committed support in appendix.

☐   5. Includes all resources, not just cash.

☐   6. Does not count on unsecured grant funds.

Recollecting with
tears how, in earlier years,
it had taken no pains
with its sums.

LEWIS CARROLL
The Hunting of the Snark

Budget
What Will It Cost? Who Will Pay?

The budget is an estimate of the resources it will take to operate your organization's program and shows how those resources will be used. The quality of thought that you give to budget preparation will not only produce a better program, it will also increase your chances of obtaining the grant.

If your brain freezes when you hear the word "budget," take heart. If you can use the main functions of a calculator and produce basic documents with a computer spreadsheet program, that's all you'll need. You don't have to be a mathematician.

Plan the Budget as You Plan the Program

Grant dollars may be the primary source of support for a program, but additional cash and donated goods and services are usually needed as well. As you begin planning the program, create a simple spreadsheet to capture your calculations for the resources the program will need and how those resources will be allocated.

Break the budget into three categories:

- Grant Request
- Other Cash Resources
- In-Kind Donations.

Then, as you identify each specific resource needed, establish a line in the spreadsheet (called a line item) and show what cash or in-kind resource will cover it. Keep detailed notes each step of the way showing how you calculated expenses and where you expect additional cash and in-kind resources to come from.

Update the spreadsheet as the planning moves along. Working this way will make it much easier to produce a final budget.

Budget
may also be called

line-item budget
program expenses
resources needed

Here's an example of what a working spreadsheet might look like. The line items you'll include will depend on the specific needs of the program.

BUDGET ITEM	GRANT REQUEST	OTHER CASH	IN-KIND	TOTAL
PERSONNEL				
Salaries & Wages				
1)				
2)				
3)				
Add line items as needed				
Subtotal Salaries & Wages				
Payroll taxes and fringe benefits @____%				
Subtotal Personnel Salaries & Wages plus Benefits				
NON-PERSONNEL EXPENSES Materials & Services				
1)				
2)				
3)				
Add line items as needed				
Subtotal Non-Personnel				
TOTAL Direct Expenses Personnel plus Non-Personnel				
Indirect Expense @____% **of Total Direct Expense**				
TOTAL PROGRAM EXPENSE Direct Exp. plus Indirect Exp.				

Budgeting Basics

Involve senior managers during planning stage. During early planning, many budget dilemmas rear their heads. It may turn out that the most promising funder won't pay indirect expenses. Or total costs may be higher than expected, setting off a scramble for additional resources to avoid scaling back the program. Managers who have not been included in the planning may surprise everyone with critical questions at the last minute, putting the entire venture in jeopardy.

Follow directions exactly. Some funders let applicants use budget formats of their own choosing. Others are quite strict. If a funder asks your organization to use a certain budget format or specific forms, do it. If the funder asks that requests not exceed $25,000, do not ask for $25,001. If instructions seem unclear, ask the funder for clarification.

It's got to add up! Take great care that the budget's numbers add up (and down and across). Double-check the spreadsheet numbers on a calculator to make sure no one entered the wrong figures or used incorrect formulas.

Sync it with the narrative and keep numbers consistent. The budget document should tell the same story as the Methods and Evaluation Sections—but in the language of dollars. Every line item in the budget must reflect the proposal narrative. And every item or activity described in the narrative that will require cash or in-kind resources must show up in the budget.

When making a last-minute change to the budget, it's easy to forget to change the figures in the cover letter and proposal summary. Be careful. This mistake is common. If the budget figures aren't consistent throughout the proposal, it's confusing and you lose credibility.

Include everything. It's critical to detail all expected resources and revenues, and itemize all cash and in-kind resources the program will consume. Be detailed. Don't overlook anything.

What happens if money is budgeted to buy a van but nothing is included for gas, insurance, and maintenance? Mistakes like this could leave your organization short on cash with lots of the program still to run.

When all income and expenses are shown, the funder can see how its grant fits into the larger budget picture—something every funder wants to know.

Be specific—itemize. As with the words in your proposal, the numbers should be as specific as possible. It's not enough to list personnel expenses at $150,000. Break it down by itemizing each employee position, the percentage of each position dedicated to the program, and the funds allocated for each position.

It's not good enough to indicate that computer equipment will cost $10,500. Specify each piece of equipment or software to be purchased, along with its cost and the function it will serve. Funders want to know exactly what their money will buy and for what it will be used.

Although estimates must be as precise as possible, it's not necessary to include the pennies. Round off to the nearest dollar or maybe $10, but not to the nearest $100.

Bulletproof estimates. Take the time to estimate exactly what each line item in the budget will cost. Don't guess. Base estimates on quotes and price checks. Doing it right will protect against estimates that are too low or too high and will minimize the need for changes once the program is under way.

For example, if the program coordinator must travel to a national conference, don't accept someone's speculation that the trip will cost $1,500. Do the research. A little time on the Internet might show that costs will be $650 for air fare, $60 for taxi fares ($30 x 2 trips), $800 for hotel ($200/night x 4 nights), and $360 per diem ($60/day x 6 days). When this kind of research is done, it's not uncommon to find that costs are higher than expected. In this case, a better estimate would be $1,870.

Keep notes on how you came up with the estimates. You may need them later for discussions with the funder.

Planning minimizes adjustments later. Funders understand that budgets are estimates, and most will allow some latitude in exactly how grant dollars are spent.

There's usually some flexibility with moving funds between line items. But doing the same between expense categories (e.g., between equipment and personnel) can be difficult—you usually have to plead your case. Inserting new line items is often forbidden, and the amount of the grant is seldom increased.

Find out what changes require the funder's prior approval and ask for clarification if in doubt. Once the program is under way, any request for a budget change should be made in writing, and the funder should respond in writing. The funder's written approval of the change is a "budget modification" that changes the conditions of the grant.

Be reasonable. The budget should honestly reflect the costs of doing business in the area where the program will operate. Don't pad it in anticipation that the funder will offer less than your organization requests. Don't pad it for any reason. If the budget is solid but the grant award is less than requested, discuss possible options with the funder. The choice may be to scale down the program or find additional sources of support.

But don't strip the budget to bare bones in hopes of making the proposal more attractive. If the budget is so lean that it cannot support the weight of the program, how can your organization deliver what is promised? Keep it real.

Have an expert review it. If your organization doesn't have a financial manager or bookkeeper, find a board member or volunteer experienced with finances. Whoever reviews the budget should understand finances well enough to spot issues that could raise questions. Your expert should also review the proposal narrative to make sure there's no disconnect with the budget.

An incomplete, inaccurate, inconsistent, or sloppy budget can be a deal killer. It makes you look like you don't know what you're doing.

Follow the Rules

Your organization has ground rules for budgeting. Whether they are written policies or unwritten expectations that have evolved over time, they exist. Who in your organization has to approve the final budget? Must indirect expense be covered? Is there a way to handle grants that reimburse expenses rather than pay up front? Find someone who knows the rules and follow them strictly.

Foundations and corporations usually provide minimal information about how to construct a budget. Most will state how large an award they will consider. Some list expenses they won't cover. Some give guidance about indirect expenses and matching resources, but most don't.

State, county, and local governments usually issue separate guidelines for each funding competition. Their budget guidance is likely to be specific, with many dos and don'ts.

Federal agencies issue guidelines for each grant competition that specify budget parameters and format. When a grant competition has specialized requirements about how funds can and can't be used, the guidelines will lay those out. But circulars issued by the Office of Management and Budget (OMB) are where you'll find the heavy-duty guidance you need. If you'll be constructing budgets for federal grant programs, you or someone else within your organization must be familiar with the OMB circulars.

The OMB circulars explain cost principles (what's allowable and what's not when spending grant funds) and administrative requirements (how grant funds should be managed once awarded). There are different circulars for different types of organizations, and they address countless questions. What are the acceptable uses of earned income? What's the difference between equipment and supplies? When are bids required for purchases or consultants? Can grant funds be used to pay entertainment expenses?

The circulars also address broader budget concerns. Federal grant funds, for example, are meant to supplement existing funding rather than supplant it. Let's say a grant recipient uses federal funds to pay a staff member for work that was previously funded from that organization's operating budget.

Now suppose that the organization uses the freed-up operating dollars to support other organizational functions. That's supplanting. It's not allowed.

OMB circulars are available online at www.whitehouse.gov/omb/circulars.

Budgets for Collaborative Programs

If a program will include significant collaboration with other organizations, you'll want the budget to reflect those partnerships.

Show partner contributions. Make sure the budget shows how the resources provided by partner groups will contribute to the operation of the program. Contributions of staff time, space, or equipment from partners will be allocated as matching resources— either cash or in-kind.

You can format the line-item budget to show a column for each contributing partner. Or you can use just one column for the total of partner contributions, and then use the budget justification to explain what's being contributed by whom.

Funding may be shared. Grantees often share the grant funds with partner organizations. The mechanism to

formalize these financial relationships can range from a simple letter of agreement to a contract or a subgrant.

Depending on the amount of money involved and the complexity of the project, you might want to attach a line-item budget from partner groups showing how they will spend the pass-through grant funds. You might also want to attach a copy of the contract or sub-grant that will govern their financial relationship with your organization.

The same rules apply. When working collaboratively with partner organizations, the same rules that govern your organization's use of grant funds must also govern their use of the pass-through grant funds you provide. Be sure partner organizations understand the dos and don'ts of the funding. Put the rules in writing or provide them with copies of the guidance you receive from the funder.

Anatomy of the Budget

The outline below illustrates how program budgets are typically organized in three parts: the budget summary, the detailed line-item budget, and the budget justification. A more detailed explanation of each part follows this outline, and a full example of a budget and budget justification begins on page 167.

I. BUDGET SUMMARY

- Summarizes all revenues and resources that will support the program
- Summarizes all expenses, showing how both cash and in-kind resources are allocated
- Is generally presented before the detailed line-item budget

II. DETAILED LINE-ITEM BUDGET

- Addresses all aspects of the budget, including revenues and resources, direct expenses, and indirect expenses
- Expenses are generally divided into two categories: direct and indirect
- How expenses are calculated may be shown here or in the budget justification

Revenues & Resources: Shows specific allocation of all requested funds, other cash, and in-kind contributions

Expenses

1. Direct expenses: Expenses directly attributable to program operation and generally broken into two categories: personnel and non-personnel

Personnel includes:
- a line item for the salary or wages of each position in the program
- fringe benefits
- the value of volunteer time

Non-personnel includes:
- all expenses other than salaries, wages and benefits
- categories such as contracted services, facilities, equipment, travel, supplies, other expenses

Total direct expenses: All direct expense line items

2. Indirect expenses: Expenses not directly attributable to program (for example, the annual organizational audit)

- May or may not be allowed by funder
- Are calculated as a percentage of total direct expenses
- Are presented as a total sum rather than broken into line items

TOTAL program expenses: Direct expenses plus indirect expenses

III. BUDGET JUSTIFICATION

- A narrative describing expenses, clarifying how they relate to the program
- May be separate from or incorporated into the line-item budget
- Shows how expenses are calculated, if that information is not detailed in the line-item budget

Budget Summary

The budget summary is a chart or simple spreadsheet that gives an overview of where resources will come from and how they'll be used. It shows the funds and in-kind resources that each contributor will provide, as well as the total for each of the budget's major expense categories. The budget summary, like the proposal summary, is written after the budget is complete and is presented at the beginning of the budget.

Detailed Line-Item Budget

A detailed line-item budget is a chart or spreadsheet giving a nitty-gritty explanation of the working parts of a budget: revenues and resources, direct expenses, and indirect expenses.

REVENUES AND RESOURCES

Most grants don't cover all costs associated with a program, and it's important to tell the funder where the other resources will come from. Including additional cash and in-kind resources in the program budget indicates support from others and shows that the total value of the program will be more than the amount of the grant request.

Because award decisions are based on the logic of the total budget, not just the portion requested from the funder, the additional cash and in-kind resources you include in the budget are a commitment. If these additional resources have not been secured, indicate that in the revenue summary at the beginning of the budget.

Additional cash. Cash may come from other grants, partner organizations, fees for services, earned income, donations, fundraising events, or your organization's unrestricted funds. The cash doesn't have to come directly to your organization. For example, a donor might pay rent for the program's facilities directly to the landlord. Or a mental health center might pay its psychologist to lead the program's parent discussion group.

In-kind resources. Goods and services that are provided free of charge are called in-kind resources. Though they are free, they still have a cash value. When a sports shop lets a youth group use its rental snowboards

for a day but doesn't charge a fee, that's an in-kind donation. The value of that donation is the shop's established daily rental rate multiplied by the number of snowboards used. In-kind resources are a great source of support. Just be sure your organization's estimate of the value is grounded in reality.

Volunteers. Volunteers provide a substantial part of the workforce for some programs, and the value of their time can add up to a large in-kind donation. Calculate the value of volunteer hours by using the rate paid for similar work within your organization or the rate commonly paid in the community for comparable services.

Base the value of volunteer time on the service provided, not on the credentials of the volunteer. For example, the time of a brain surgeon serving meals at a soup kitchen must be valued at the rate paid to an entry-level kitchen worker. But if the doctor donates surgical services, that time is valued at the fee commonly paid to a brain surgeon.

After establishing an hourly rate for a volunteer, you may increase it by the percentage your organization uses to calculate fringe benefits for employees. If the hourly rate of an entry-level kitchen worker is $10 and your organization pays 23% in fringe benefits, the hourly value of the brain surgeon serving soup would be $12.30.

The federal Office of Management and Budget provides guidance for calculating the value of volunteer time in Circular A-110 (Subpart C.23). Other sources calculate the average hourly value of volunteer time for specific locales, but the numbers may not be a good fit. Using figures tailored to your community and circumstances will produce the most defensible estimate.

Documentation. This is critical because additional cash and in-kind resources don't exist to an auditor unless they're documented. If a donor gives a landlord the rent check, your organization must secure documentation proving the transaction took place and benefited the program. Require volunteers to sign time sheets documenting the hours they contribute and get a receipt marked "donation" from the store donating use of the snowboards. Documenting some in-kind donations can be more complicated, like the on-and-off use of an old office computer. Before including such a contribution in the budget, consider the documentation required.

Matching Resources

When funders require that the budget include additional cash or in-kind donations, they usually use the term "matching resources" or simply "match."

Be realistic about the match your organization can generate. Government funders may require that some portion of a grant be returned if the promised match fails to materialize. With private funders, failing to generate promised match can damage your organization's reputation.

Most federal agencies require nonfederal match. That means they won't accept funds from other federal sources as match, even if those funds are passed through local or state agencies. Some funders will accept only cash match, but many will accept in-kind match as well.

Cash match may also be called "hard match." For a match to be considered cash, someone must pay for something—money must change hands.

In-kind match may also be called "soft match." For a match to be considered in-kind, the goods or services must have value, even though no money changes hands.

All match must be integral to the program's operation. It must legitimately contribute to the program.

Matching Resources
may also be called
· ·

cost share

leveraged resources

local contribution

match

matching funds

nonfederal contribution

nonfederal share

other support

BE SURE TO USE THE RIGHT CALCULATION FOR MATCH

Some funders require that the match be a minimum percentage of the grant request. When they do, be sure your organization understands whether that minimum percentage must be based on the amount of the *grant request* alone or on the *total program budget.*

This distinction is critical. The total program budget is not just the grant request. It's the grant request plus all matching resources.

If the funder requires that the minimum match be based on the total program budget but your organization bases it on the grant request alone, that mistake could disqualify the grant proposal.

> **Funder #1—grant request only:** The requested grant amount is $100,000. This funder requires a minimum match of 10% of the requested grant. This calculation is simple: $100,000 grant request multiplied by 10% required match equals $10,000 minimum match. In this scenario, the $100,000 grant request plus the $10,000 minimum match equals a minimum total program budget of $110,000.

> **Funder #2—total program budget:** The requested grant amount is $100,000. The funder requires a minimum match of 10% of the total program budget and will pay only 90% of the total program budget. This calculation is more complex. Multiply the requested grant amount of $100,000 times the 10% rate of match, then divide by 90% (the percentage of the budget the funder is willing to support) to get the required minimum match of $11,111. In this scenario, the $100,000 grant request plus the $11,111 minimum match equals a minimum total program budget of $111,111.

EXPENSES

1. Direct Expenses

This category includes costs directly attributable to operation of the program, and costs are listed as either personnel or non-personnel.

PERSONNEL EXPENSES

These include salaries, wages, fringe benefits, and the value of volunteer time.

Salaries and wages. Create a line item for each person who will be employed or otherwise involved in the program.

- For salaried employees, multiply their annual salary by the percentage of time they will dedicate to the program.

- For volunteers, multiply the appropriate hourly rate by the number of hours they will dedicate to the program.

Watch percentages. Supervisors are often paid from several funding sources. Unless you keep track of which funder is paying for what percentage of which position, there could be a problem. Your organization could end up being compensated for more than 100% of a manager's time, an error that would surface in the annual financial audit.

Count everyone. A grant-funded program often requires time from many employees.

An administrative assistant may enter monthly data. The executive director may supervise the program coordinator. The van driver may add a new route, just for the program.

If the grant will not pay an appropriate percentage of an employee's time, be sure to capture that time as a cash contribution—a cash match.

Pay raises. In a multiyear budget, account for annual pay raises, if your organization routinely gives them.

The salary scale. If you know that a new position will be filled at either the low or high end of the salary scale, budget for that. If you don't know, it's practical to budget at the midpoint.

Stick with personnel policies. Employees paid from grant funds must receive the same benefits as employees paid by other means. But what if the terms of the grant do not allow for vacation time, sick time, or other benefits normally provided by your organization? In that case, such expenses must be paid by the organization itself, which can budget them as a cash contribution to the program.

Fringe benefits. All employers must pay workers' compensation insurance and unemployment insurance, and must contribute to their employees' Social Security and Medicare benefit payments (FICA) as well. Most organizations also pay for other employee benefits such as health insurance, dental insurance, disability insurance and the like.

Benefits are generally calculated as a percentage of salaries and wages. That percentage depends on the benefits offered—the more benefits, the higher the fringe rate. Some funders will want to see a breakdown of that fringe rate. For example, what makes up a 25% fringe rate? How much of that is health insurance? Disability? Dental plan? Other funders will want to see only the total percentage, plus a list of the benefits provided.

If a funder doesn't say exactly what information to include, be as thorough as possible. Your grant proposal can lose points if a funder is left with unanswered questions.

NON-PERSONNEL EXPENSES

These include costs directly associated with program operations. Typical categories are contracted services, facilities, equipment, supplies, travel and other expenses. These categories are broad and are generally adequate for all budgets.

Contractual services. People who are paid to provide services but who are not employees are contractors, often called consultants. Contracting for services can be an efficient, cost-effective way to get things done. Even if the hourly or daily charge is high, services are generally short-term, and your organization doesn't pay fringe benefits.

Contractors are paid by the day, the hour, or the job. Some funders limit a contractor's daily rate, so be aware of each funder's rules.

Who's a contractor and who's an employee? The Internal Revenue Service (IRS) takes a great deal of interest in that question, and IRS publication 15-A, Employer's Supplemental Tax Guide, spells out the difference.

Whether or not your organization calls someone a contractor doesn't matter to the IRS. What matters is the degree of independence that individual has in performing the work. In most cases, an individual who has little or no independence must be treated as an employee. Your organization should never try to avoid paying benefits by classifying an employee as a contractor. Penalties from the IRS for such behavior can be severe.

Facilities. To calculate the cost of space for the program, multiply the amount of space you will use by a cost per square foot that is aligned with fair market rates. Be sure to include the cost of heat, air-conditioning, electricity, water, insurance, cleaning, and maintenance.

If your organization will operate the program in its own facility, you can count that contribution as match (cash, if your organization rents, or in-kind, if it owns), or you can ask the funder to pay for use of the space. When calculating cash or in-kind match, don't forget to consider facilities donated by collaborating organizations.

Equipment. The federal government defines equipment as a tangible item that will last more than a year and costs more than $5,000. To the federal government, most computers are consumable supplies, as are desks, chairs, and conference tables. Unlike the feds, most foundations and corporations expect to see computers and office furniture as line items within the equipment category. Be sure you understand the requirements of the funder to whom you're applying.

When the grant-funded program will make use of your organization's equipment—or that of a collaborator—the value can be claimed as in-kind match. For example, using six canoes for two days can be valued at the standard cost of renting them. If the program will have the dedicated use of a computer, your organization can calculate the value by determining the cost of renting or buying a similar computer. But if the program will share the computer with others, it's fair to claim only a percentage of that value. Because all matching resources must be documented, record-keeping for a shared computer might be more trouble than it's worth.

Supplies. They are consumable—they get used up. General office supplies are the most common example: pens, paper, tape, and printer cartridges. Use your organization's experience to estimate an annual expense for each person working or volunteering in the program. If your organization is new, ask people at other organizations about their experience.

Cost estimates must be more exact when it comes to other types of supplies. When budgeting for training manuals, for example, specify the manual's title, how many copies the program will need and how much each will cost. Calculate how many pounds of clay the pottery class will use each month and multiply that by the cost per pound and the number of months the program will operate.

Travel. Budgets often divide travel expenses into two categories: local and non-local. Local travel, which excludes the employee's commute, is travel that can be completed in one day, without an overnight stay. Employers generally pay a set amount per mile (mileage) when staff members use personal vehicles for business. Mileage payments are the most common local travel expense, but fares for bus, train, taxi, or even air travel can also fall into this category.

Non-local travel is travel that cannot be completed within one day. Typical nonlocal travel expenses include mileage payments, air fares, rental cars, taxi fares, hotel accommodations, and per diem allowances.

Per diem means "per day" in Latin and is generally a lump sum payment for an employee's daily living expenses while on the road. It can be spent on meals, laundry service, and other personal needs. Per diem may sometimes be paid for local travel, but it is always paid for nonlocal travel.

Other expenses. This captures expenses that don't fit into any of the other five categories. But it is not a catchall for vaguely defined contingencies or undefined miscellaneous expenses. Miscellaneous expenses have no place in the program budget. The expenses listed here must meet a well-defined program need.

The following line items are commonly included as other expenses:

- telephone and communications (land lines, cellphones, Internet connections)

- professional development

- books and periodicals

- copying and printing

- mailing (postage and express delivery)

- insurance that relates specifically to the program

- client activities (entry fees, group transportation, equipment rental)

- food (meals in a residential program, snacks in an after-school program, refreshments for a training program)

- professional memberships.

2. Indirect Expenses

Each grant-funded program is dependent upon your organization's infrastructure. For example, the annual audit, the salaries of the bookkeeper and receptionist, general liability insurance, building maintenance, and general technology updates are essential to all of your organization's programs yet difficult to attribute directly to any one specific program. Every program has to carry an appropriate portion of these necessary yet indirect expenses. The budget category called "indirect expenses" captures these costs. Indirect expenses are generally calculated as a percentage of each program's direct expenses and included in each program's budget as a lump sum, rather than by line item.

Some funders require that contractual expenses and equipment be subtracted from the direct expenses total before applying the agreed upon percentage for calculating indirect expenses. As always, read instructions carefully and contact the funder if you're confused. In the example that begins on page 167, contractual costs are subtracted from Total Direct Expense before the indirect expense rate is applied, as shown on page 175.

Support varies. Some foundations and corporations will support only a minimal amount of indirect expense—perhaps 5% or 10% of direct expense. And many won't support indirect expenses at all. Local, county, and state governments will generally support indirect expenses, but only if the request is modest, perhaps 10% to 15% of direct expense. Even though you have to jump through a lot of hoops to establish a negotiated indirect cost rate with the federal government, the amount that the federal agencies will actually pay varies by funding program.

When a funder will not support indirect expenses—or not at a reasonable rate—your organization must cover that cost itself. The time required to administer the program might be absorbed by the regular administrative staff, or a search could be undertaken for additional funds. In any event, carefully examine the real costs of implementing a program. If a grant will not support indirect expenses, can your organization really afford to operate the program?

Some don't use indirect. Some organizations choose not to use indirect expenses as a budget category. Instead, they methodically calculate the portion of an infrastructure-related activity that can be claimed as a program expense. Then they budget it as a direct expense line item.

For example, an organization might argue that it can identify the portion of a receptionist's time that will be devoted to the grant-funded program and then budget that portion of time as a direct expense. In this case, the organization must keep meticulous records. If one day a week of the receptionist's time is charged to the grant as a direct expense, payroll records must verify that the receptionist spent one day a week doing work directly for the program.

Indirect Expenses
may also be called
· ·

administrative expenses

administrative overhead

operating overhead

This is the approach an organization might use when submitting a proposal to funders who won't pay indirect expenses. It's generally acceptable if the basis for the calculation is clear and defensible and if a direct relationship between the expenditure and the program is documented.

Negotiating with the feds. As of January 2015, applicants for federal grants can include a minimal 10% indirect rate in budgets–no paperwork required. But to request a higher amount that's more in keeping with your organization's actual costs, you'll need a negotiated indirect cost rate agreement.

Negotiated rates vary tremendously, but 25% to 35% of direct expenses is not unusual, and for some large, complex institutions, rates exceed 50%. Once a final indirect

166 GRANTSMANSHIP: PROGRAM PLANNING & PROPOSAL WRITING

cost rate agreement has been negotiated, it is accepted by all federal agencies (unless prohibited by statute).

But not every competition allows indirect costs to be paid at the full rate. When your organization can't recover its established rate, some federal agencies allow the difference between what you can request and your established rate to be claimed as match.

When first applying for a negotiated rate, an organization usually submits paperwork to the same agency to which it's applying for grant funds. Approved rates are good for between one and three years, so you'll have to renegotiate within the required time frame to maintain a current agreement.

You'll find detailed guidance in the federal Office of Management and Budget Super Circular (technically called "Uniform Administrative Requirements, Cost Principles, and Audit Requirements for Federal Awards") published December 26, 2013, in the Federal Register (Vol. 78, No. 248, pages 78589–78691). The permanent home for this information is the Code of Federal Regulations (CFR). Look for 2 CFR Subpart E Cost Principles, and Appendices III-IX for guidance for various types of organizations. The Grantsmanship Center also offers an in-depth article titled "What You Need to Know About Indirect Costs." Visit tgci.com and look under Publications.

Budget Justification

A budget justification is an explanation of how your organization calculated budget expenses and how line items relate to program operations. It's easy for funders to forget important program details by the time they get around to reading the proposed budget, even when the narrative and budget are well coordinated. A succinct budget justification increases the odds that funders will understand why every expense is reasonable and necessary.

When funders require a budget justification, some will ask that each line item be explained while others will accept a general discussion by category. Some may ask for justification of any expense that raises questions.

A budget justification should:

- explain the expenses required to operate the program

- show how each cost is calculated (if not defined in the line-item budget)

- show how the value of in-kind resources is calculated (if not defined in the line-item budget)

- explain where other cash and in-kind resources will come from and note whether these resources are anticipated or secured.

In some budget formats, detailed cost calculations are included in line items. In others, the calculations are shown in the budget justification. Just be sure the cost calculations show up in one place or the other.

Justification vs. narrative. The terms "budget justification" and "budget narrative" are usually interchangeable, but not always. In rare cases, funders will require both a budget justification and a narrative. When both are requested, the budget narrative usually addresses the broad issues raised by the budget: Is this a good investment? Are there special circumstances that make line items higher or lower? Adding up the total budget, what is the cost per participant or unit of service, and is that cost reasonable? The budget justification, on the other hand, provides detailed information on particular line items.

If in doubt about how the funder defines these terms, ask for clarification.

EXAMPLE: BUDGET

This budget, presented in traditional line-item format, covers the first year of a family services program called *Learning to Succeed*. Its target population is troubled young people, and mentoring is an important part of the program. All positions, except the clinical administrator, are new and time is allowed for recruiting and hiring. The value of volunteer time is included as in-kind match. The budget justification is included as a separate document.

Learning to Succeed—Year One Program Budget

BUDGET SUMMARY

SUMMARY: Revenues & Resources – Year 1		Notes
Helping Hand Foundation	262,254	Requested
Family Services unrestricted funds	4,095	Committed by board on 6/10/2014
In-kind donations	29,840	Volunteers & volunteer travel to be secured. Space and food committed.
TOTAL Year 1	**296,189**	

SUMMARY: Expenses by Major Category – Year 1

Expenses	Grant Request	Matching Resources	Total
Personnel	163,275	23,295	186,570
Contractual services	25,000		25,000
Facilities	5,750	2,000	7,750
Equipment	10,820		10,820
Travel	9,000	7,200	16,200
Supplies	2,000		2,000
Other expense	24,840	1,440	26,280
Total direct expense	240,685	33,935	274,620
Indirect expense @ 10%	21,569		21,569
TOTAL Year 1	**262,254**	**33,935**	**296,189**

LINE-ITEM BUDGET

DIRECT EXPENSE

Personnel Expense	Grant Request	Match	Total
(1) Program director: 1 FTE at $45,000, 11 months in year 1	41,250		41,250
(2) Counselors: 2 FTEs at $35,000, 10 months in year 1	58,333		58,333
(3) Clinical administrator: 5% FTE at salary of $65,000		3,250	3,250
(4) Volunteer coordinator: 60% FTE at salary of $30,000, 10 months in year 1	15,000		15,000
(5) Clerical support: 60% FTE at salary of $25,000	15,000		15,000
(6) Volunteer: 20 mentors x 2 hrs/wk x 32 weeks x $15/hr		19,200	19,200
Fringe Benefits			
(7) Calculated at 26% of salary. Volunteers excluded	33,692	845	34,537
Subtotal Personnel Expense	**163,275**	**23,295**	**186,570**

Non-Personnel Expense	Grant Request	Match	Total
Contractual Services Expense			
(8) Evaluation consultant: contracted rate for completion of all evaluation tasks	25,000		25,000
Facilities Expense			
(9) Office facilities: 5 staff x 50 square feet each x rental rate of $23/square foot/year	5,750		5,750
(10) Youth activity night meeting space: gymnasium at $125 night x 2 nights/month x 8 months		2,000	2,000
Subtotal Facilities Expense	**5,750**	**2,000**	**7,750**
Equipment Expense			
(11) Office equipment: desk ($600), chair ($300), file cabinet ($150), cellphone ($50). $1,100 x 5 staff	5,500		5,500
(12) Laptop computers and software at $1,330 x 4 staff	5,320		5,320
Subtotal Equipment Expense	**10,820**		**10,820**
Travel Expense			
(13) Local travel: estimated at 8,000 miles in year 1, paid at .45/mile	3,600		3,600
(14) Non-local travel: 3 staff members to conference in Washington, DC @ $1,800 each	5,400		5,400
15) Volunteer local travel: estimated at 16,000 miles in year 1, valued at .45/mile		7,200	7,200
Subtotal Travel Expense	**9,000**	**7,200**	**16,200**

Non-Personnel Expense - continued	Grant Request	Match	Total
Supplies Expense			
(16) Office supplies: consumable office supplies estimated at $300/year x 5 staff	1,500		1,500
(17) Volunteer training manuals: $25 per manual x 20 volunteers	500		500
Subtotal Supplies Expense	**2,000**		**2,000**
Other Expense			
(18) Copying: 6,000 copies per year at .05 per copy	300		300
(19) Communication: phone $50/month; Internet $50/month; cellphones $200/month. Total $300 per month x 12 months	3,600		3,600
(20) Postage & express delivery: based on agency experience: $75/month x 12 months	900		900
(21) Youth activities: estimated at $1,700/ month x 8 months in year 1	13,600		13,600
(22) Snacks for youth groups: 36 groups in year 1 x 20 youths x $4/youth.	1,440	1,440	2,880
(23) Staff development: $1,000 per year x 5 staff	5,000		5,000
Subtotal Other Expense	**24,840**	**1,440**	**26,280**
TOTAL All Direct Expense	240,685	33,935	274,620
INDIRECT EXPENSE: calculated at 10% of qualifying direct expense	21,569		21,569
TOTAL ALL EXPENSES	**262,254**	**33,935**	**296,189**

BUDGET JUSTIFICATION

Direct Expenses

Personnel

(1) Program director: *1 FTE at $45,000, 11 months in year 1 = $41,250. Supervised by clinical administrator. Job description in appendix, page 15. Responsible for day-to-day operation of program, including supervision of staff, participation in evaluation, reporting, serving as liaison with school and community, and assisting in direct service. One month allowed for recruitment and hiring.*

(2) Counselors: *2 FTEs at $35,000 each, ten months each in year 1 = $58,333. Supervised by program director. Job description in appendix, page 16. Will implement youth skill-building groups and activity nights, provide training and support to volunteers, and provide individual and group counseling to youths. Two months allowed for recruitment and hiring.*

(3) Supervision by clinical administrator: *5% FTE at salary of $65,000 = $3,250. Dr. Chatura Patel, Clinical Administrator, is supervised by the Family Service Agency's executive director. Dr. Patel's résumé and the job description for her work in this program are in the appendix, pages 17 and 18. She will supervise the program director, monitor clinical records, provide consultation to counseling staff, and oversee client referral to additional psychological services as needed. Expense will be a cash donation from agency's unrestricted funds.*

(4) Volunteer coordinator: *60% FTE at salary of $30,000, ten months in year 1 = $15,000. Supervised by program director. Job description in appendix, page 19. Responsible for volunteer recruitment, screening, training, scheduling, supervision, and recognition. Two months allowed for recruitment and hiring.*

(5) Clerical support: *60% FTE at salary of $25,000 = $15,000. Supervised by program director. Job description in appendix, page 20. Will establish and manage database, prepare volunteer materials, track volunteer time, maintain files, and perform other logistical and organizational tasks as needed. Agency experience indicates position can be filled in month 1.*

(6) Volunteer mentors: *Donation of time valued at $19,200. Role description in appendix, page 21. Volunteer time valued at a total of $15/hour. $13.40/hour value is equivalent to annual salary of $27,800, which is the average salary the agency pays a trained youth activity leader. $1.60/hour (12%) is added to represent the value of basic fringe benefits. Volunteers will serve 32 weeks (8 months) in year 1. The in-kind value of this resource is calculated at 20 volunteers x 2 hours/week x 32 weeks x $15/hour = $19,200.*

(7) Fringe benefits: *$34,537. The agency pays benefits for employees who are 60% FTE or more. Benefits are calculated at 26% of salary and include FICA 7.65%; unemployment insurance 2.9%; workers' compensation 1%; health insurance 12%; life and disability insurance 1%; and dental benefit 1.45%. The agency will contribute benefits for the clinical administrator's time on this program.*

Contractual Services

(8) Evaluation: *$25,000. The program evaluation will be conducted by the Center for Suburban Research. The résumé of Dr. Bernard Rousseau, lead evaluator, is on page 26 of the appendix. This contract will include all aspects of implementing the evaluation plan. This contractual expense is subtracted from Total Direct Expense before applying the indirect cost rate.*

Facilities

(9) Office facilities: *$5,750. This expense covers rent, heat, utilities, and maintenance and is calculated at 5 staff members x 50 square feet of space each x $23/year per square foot. $23/square foot is the average annual cost of renting office space in our county.*

(10) Youth activity meeting space: *$2,000. The city Recreation Department will donate use of its gymnasium twice each month. The gym is handicapped accessible, spacious, has adequate restrooms, and has an attached kitchen. The value of this donation is calculated at 2 nights per month x 8 months x $125/night (cost of renting the space).*

Equipment

(11) Office equipment: *$5,500. The 5 new staff members will be provided with desks (5 @ $600 = $3,000); chairs (5 @ $300 = $1,500); file cabinets (5 @ $150 = $750); and cell phones (5 @ $50 = $250). Discount Cell Communications, Inc.*

provided price quotes for cellphones, and Office Warehouse provided quotes for furniture of mid-level quality. The equipment cost for each staff member will total $1,100.

*(12) **Computers:** $5,320. The clerical assistant will use an agency desktop computer. Laptops are required for the 4 other staff who will frequently engage in tasks outside the office. The cost of a major computer corporation laptop with wireless technology, a CD drive, and software is quoted at $1,330. Staff will use printers available at the agency's office.*

Travel

*(13) **Local travel:** $3,600. Staff will travel approximately 8,000 miles in year 1 to provide counseling, support volunteers, implement activities, and attend hearings, trainings, and meetings. Mileage is paid at .45/mile.*

*(14) **Non-local travel:** $5,400. The program director and two counselors will attend the Life Skills Conference in Washington, D.C., sponsored by the National Healthy Children Coalition. This conference is noted for high-quality training. Costs are calculated as follows: air fare for 3 @ $650 = $1,950; hotel room @ $200/night x 3 staff x 4 nights = $2,400; per diem @ $60/day x 3 staff x 5 days = $900; taxi travel during conference estimated at $50 x 3 staff = $150. The total cost for each staff member will be $1,800.*

*(15) **Volunteer local travel:** $7,200. Each volunteer will travel approximately 25 miles/week for training, events, and mentoring. Costs for the projected 16,000 miles of travel in year 1 will be donated by the volunteers. The value of this donation is calculated at 20 volunteers x 32 weeks x 25 miles/week x .45/mile.*

Supplies

*(16) **Office supplies:** $1,500. Agency experience indicates that each staff member will require $300/year in office supplies. This includes all consumables (paper, ink cartridges, notebooks, filing equipment, small desktop appliances, pens, clips, sticky notes, etc.).*

*(17) **Volunteer training manuals:** $500. Each volunteer will receive The Mentoring Manual ($25) published by the Mentoring for the Future Foundation. Selection of this resource is discussed on page 8 of the proposal and the expense is calculated at 20 volunteers x $25.*

Other Expenses

(18) Copying: *$300. Estimated at 6,000 copies in year 1 for volunteer materials, planning documents, evaluation materials, reports, letters, forms, etc. Copies will be charged at the standard business rate of $.05 each.*

(19) Communication: *$3,600. Land-line phone service for 5 staff is estimated at a total of $50/month. The program's Internet connection will cost $50/month. Cellphone service at $50/month for 4 staff will cost $200/month. The total cost of communication is estimated at $300/month. Savings from staff vacancies in months 1 and 2 will cover start-up fees.*

(20) Postage and express delivery: *$900. Agency experience indicates the program will need $23/month for postage and $52/month for express mail delivery (2 packages/month at $26).*

(21) Youth activities: *$13,600.*

 (a) Mentor activities with youth: $6,400. Volunteers will be eligible for reimbursement of up to $10/week for costs incurred in mentoring (entry fees, lunch, snacks, etc.). This expense is calculated at 20 mentors x 32 weeks x $10.

 (b) Activity nights: $7,200. Program counselors will implement 2 activity nights/month. Each night will involve 45 people (20 youths, 20 mentors, 2 counselors, 3 presenters), and is budgeted at $450 for food, materials, and presenters. The cost of activity nights is calculated at 8 months in yr 1 x 2 activity nights x $450.

(22) Snacks: *$2,880. Counselors will implement 36 youth skill-building groups in year 1. Each group will serve 20 youths and include healthy snacks at an estimated cost of $4/youth. This expense is calculated at 20 youths x 36 groups x $4/youth. Wong's Friendly Market will donate groceries valued at $1,440, and the program will purchase the rest of the food.*

(23) Staff development: *$5,000. The program director and counselors will receive advanced training in counseling techniques and engaging troubled youths. The volunteer coordinator will be trained in volunteer management.*

The clerical assistant will be trained in database development and advanced spreadsheet applications. This line item is calculated at $1,000 x 5 staff members.

Indirect Expenses

$21,569. *Indirect expense will include financial management, insurance, audit, oversight by the board of directors, information technology services, receptionist services, etc. The indirect-expense request is calculated as follows:*

$240,685	*Total direct expense*
– $ 25,000	*Contractual expense*
$215,685	
x 10%	
$ 21,569	*Indirect expense request*

GLOSSARY OF BUDGET TERMS

Administrative overhead: Expenses related to the infrastructure of the applicant organization that will support the operation of the program. May also be called indirect expense or overhead expense.

Budget justification: A narrative explaining expenses and how they relate to the program. Shows how expenses were calculated, if explanation is not already presented in the line-item budget.

Budget narrative: A term often used interchangeably with budget justification, but sometimes referring to a broader discussion of the cost benefit and cost-effectiveness of the program.

Budget summary: A chart showing all revenues and resources, and all expenses, usually presented at the beginning of the budget.

Cash contributions: Money that will cover integral program expenses, but that will not come from the requested grant.

Detailed line-item budget: A chart that shows a detailed breakdown of all costs within expense categories.

Direct expense: Costs that can be directly attributed to the operation of the program.

Expense categories: Primary classifications of costs into which line items are sorted.

Full-time equivalent (FTE): The number of hours that an employee must work at an organization to be considered full-time. The hours of two or more part-time employees can make up one FTE.

Indirect expense: See Administrative Overhead.

In-kind resources: Goods and services that are integral to program operation and that are provided free of charge.

Line item: A specific cost itemized on a line within an expense category.

Matching resources: Cash, goods, or services that are integral to program operation and are provided by a source other than the requested grant. Often called match.

Negotiated indirect cost rate agreement: The mechanism the federal government uses to administer indirect costs. It defines the percentage an organization may apply to direct costs in order to calculate the amount of indirect costs allowable.

Overhead expense: See Administrative Overhead.

Subgrant: Grant funds transferred by the applicant agency to a partner organization as a means of accomplishing activities required by the grant. Sometimes refers to the written document that spells out the terms governing the use of the pass-through funds. May also be called regrant.

CHECKLIST: BUDGET

☐   1. Follows funder's directions exactly.

☐   2. Adheres to applicant organization's policies and practices.

☐   3. Is consistent with the Methods Section.

☐   4. Is consistent with the Evaluation Section.

☐   5. Is consistent with the cover letter (if included) and the proposal Summary.

☐   6. Includes a summary of all revenue, in-kind resources, and expenses.

☐   7. Itemizes resources, other than the requested grant, that will support the program (including cash and in-kind).

☐   8. Shows how cash and in-kind contributions from the funder, partner organizations, the applicant, and others will be allocated.

☐   9. Includes matching funds as required.

☐   10. Is based on solid estimates—quotes, price checks, and organizational experience.

☐   11. Is reasonable for operating the program described in the application narrative—is not too high or too low.

☐   12. Includes detailed line items for all direct-expense categories, showing calculations for each.

☐   13. Includes indirect expense (administrative overhead) whether requested or covered by other sources.

☐   14. Rationale for each budget item is clear. A budget justification is included if needed.

☐   15. Has been reviewed by an expert.

☐   16. Is accurate—the numbers add up (and down and across).

"It must be simple
in its presentation
and direct in its expression,
like the language
of Nature."

MOHANDAS GANDHI

The Send Off
Packaging and Delivering the Proposal

Resist the temptation to relax as you prepare your organization's grant proposal for delivery to a funder. It may seem that only a little tidying up remains to be done. But don't underestimate the importance of this step. How the proposal is packaged makes a big difference. For example, when a funder provides specific formatting instructions, even a small deviation can disqualify your proposal before anyone reads a single word.

Tips on Formatting

Make the proposal inviting—neat and easy to read. Funders have stacks of them to review. Anything that looks foreboding or is hard to follow will be at an immediate disadvantage. Worst of all, it may go straight into the rejection pile.

Many funders limit the number of pages they'll accept, require that pages be numbered, and specify requirements for spacing, margins, and the size and type of font. But some don't stop there. Be prepared for instructions that require original signatures in blue ink, recycled paper, two-sided copies, limited characters per inch of type, minimum space between lines, and so forth.

The cardinal rule: If a funder provides directions, follow them. Substituting your organization's ideas for the funder's requirements is disrespectful and in the worst case will disqualify your proposal.

NO INSTRUCTIONS? DO THIS:

- Single space
- Double space between paragraphs
- Use 1-inch margins all around
- Use a standard 12-point font
- Use white 8.5- by 11-inch paper
- Number all pages
- Print on only one side of pages

Understand page limits. When funders limit the number of pages a grant proposal may contain, pay attention to what is covered by the limit. It may apply only to the proposal's narrative and not to the budget, budget justification, forms, or attachments. Or it may apply to everything.

Break up the copy. Nobody wants to plod through blocks of text that fill an entire page without a break. Use subheadings, paragraph breaks, and ample spacing between lines to let the pages breathe. Aim for short paragraphs.

Headings and subheadings not only open up the text, they prepare the reader for what comes next. Short, bulleted lists break up the narrative and deliver information concisely. Numbering items or sections also helps.

Restrain yourself. When it comes to formatting, resist the impulse to be flashy. An unconventional format is risky. It may focus too much attention on the form of the proposal and detract from its content.

Select a font then stick with it. Select a standard font that's easy to read—Times Roman or Helvetica are good choices. Don't use script or anything fussy. Don't vary fonts in an attempt to emphasize a point or appear artistic. If you change fonts, do so only in headings. A hodgepodge of fonts is distracting.

Please, no shouting. Bold type, all capital letters, or underlined words can be appropriate for headings or subheadings, but avoid them within the narrative. They shout at the reader and quickly become annoying. Use italics sparingly. Edit and keep editing until the language makes your point without typographical hype.

Graphs, charts, and diagrams. Graphic elements can provide visual relief and deliver information quickly. But there's always a danger that a graphic will confound the reader no matter how hard you tried to get it right. Ask several people to look at a graphic to test whether the intended message comes through. Attach a brief explanation or caption to be sure readers get the point.

Use color cautiously. It's likely that your organization's grant proposal will be copied, and those copies probably won't be in color. If the original proposal relies on color, that could be a problem. A bar graph may become meaningless when the multicolor bars are reproduced in tones of gray. Colored section headings may lose effectiveness. Lightly colored text or graphics may vanish. Black print on white paper is always a good choice.

Edit. Don't use tricks. If the narrative is too long, don't be tempted to reduce the font size or shrink the margins. Tighten the writing instead.

Double-check with a ruler. When specific margins are required, don't just enter them into the word-processing program and consider it done. Not every printer produces

KEEP PACKAGING SIMPLE

Don't use extravagant packaging. Even when the funder has no packaging requirements for hardcopy submissions, keep it simple.

Spiral bindings were made to be cut apart and expensive covers suggest that your organization wastes money.

Instead, attach a binder clip to the top left-hand corner of the proposal to keep the pages together. Funders can easily thumb through the pages with the clip on or off.

When funders prohibit any binding, no clips or rubber bands are allowed. But don't send a stack of papers without marking where one copy stops and another begins. Place manila envelopes or sheets of brightly colored paper between copies. Or place each unbound copy in an individual file folder, then put all folders in an envelope or box.

pages to exact specifications. Print a page, measure the margins with a ruler, and adjust as necessary.

Always proofread. Typos and grammatical errors in a grant proposal undercut your proposal's credibility. Word-processing software can help, but there's no substitute for careful proofreading. "Sight," "cite" and "site" are all correct to spell-check software.

The Cover Letter

Unless a cover letter is prohibited, include one with every proposal to a foundation or corporation. With government funders, applicants are usually required to fill out a form that documents the legal authority to submit the proposal, making a cover letter unnecessary. Furthermore, many government funders count the letter against the total number of pages allowed.

An effective cover letter is brief—less than a page—and includes a concise description of the proposal. Most important, the cover letter is an opportunity to capture the funder's attention and convey your organization's firm commitment to the proposed program. If the funder has been a source of support in the past or has discussed the proposal with you in advance, be sure to express appreciation.

The cover letter from a private nonprofit organization should be signed by the chairperson of the board of directors. Even though the board may have given the executive director authority to apply for grants, it's still a good idea to have the letter come from the chairperson. If the applicant is a public nonprofit organization—a government agency, a municipality, or a school district—the letter should be signed by a high-ranking official.

Cover letters should always be printed on the applicant organization's letterhead.

Writing a cover letter may seem simple, but here are a few things to look out for:

- The cover letter is not a substitute for the proposal's Summary. If only a cover letter is submitted and it's removed or lost, the funder is at a disadvantage: there's nothing up front to summarize the proposal's contents. The Summary is vital because it's the entryway into the proposal—a cover letter can't take its place.

- Address the letter to a specific person, not "To whom it may concern" or "Dear Friend." Make sure the right person is getting the letter, spell his or her name accurately, use the correct title, and get the gender right. Finally, make sure the person is still alive. Don't rely on websites or databases or directories for this information. They can be out of date. It's safest to call the funder.

- Don't be presumptuous. Statements like "We know you will find this proposal to be of the highest significance" or "It is obvious that this program should be funded" are inappropriate.

- Don't close the letter with a flat "Call me if you have questions." Instead, seize the opportunity to open communication. Invite the funder to visit your organization or promise to follow up with a phone call.

Here's an example of a cover letter:

Trees for the City
Keeping the City Green Since 1996

January 4, 2015

Ms. Ima Caring, Senior Program Officer
City Foundation
233 North Street
Springfield, ST 51512

Dear Ms. Caring:

In the last two years, continuing urban development in Springfield has resulted in the loss of over 2,500 mature trees. To ensure that our city stays green and livable, Trees for the City works to preserve trees when possible and to replace trees that are lost. Currently, we are organizing a major campaign to plant 1,000 hardwoods by June 1, 2017.

The Rotary Club, the Springfield City Council, and the Forest Lights Foundation have pledged a total of $45,000 for the purchase of trees, fertilizer, mulch, and other planting supplies. The Lakeside Nursery is providing three- to four-foot trees at cost ($50 each) and providing free delivery to planting sites. Thirty knowledgeable volunteers, including several professional landscapers, are ready to begin planting in the spring. The city's Buildings and Grounds Department and the local Garden Club will help us tend the trees until they are well established.

The Board of Directors of Trees for the City is committed to keeping Springfield green and hopes that the City Foundation will join us and our partner organizations by providing $10,000 to complete the funding needed to purchase trees and supplies for this campaign.

I would appreciate the opportunity to discuss the campaign with you and to show you a map of planting sites. I'll call next week to see if we can set a meeting date.

Thank you for your consideration.

Sincerely,

Spiros Kostas

Spiros Kostas, Chair, Board of Directors

Attachments to the Proposal

First, find out what the funder requires and include it. If you're allowed to submit additional attachments, include only material that will inspire confidence, illustrate the problem, support the Methods Section with expanded details, or enhance the proposal in some other specific way.

Begin collecting attachments well before the submission deadline. You may need to rework the organizational chart or staff may need to update résumés. It may take a few days to get a copy of the survey from the evaluator. Letters of commitment and support often arrive later than promised, so it's a good idea to set an early deadline for receipt and give yourself time to track them down.

Here are some attachments funders frequently require:

- letters of commitment or memoranda of understanding from collaborating organizations

- most recent 990 tax return

- most recent organizational audit

- most recent monthly financial statement

- annual organizational budget

- copy of IRS Letter of Determination

- list of the board of directors, including information to demonstrate the board's diversity and quality. You might include their place of employment and job titles, the sectors of the community they represent, or even very brief bios.

- job descriptions for proposed program staffing

- résumés of key program staff who are already in place

- organizational chart for the proposed program or for the entire organization.

Here are a few examples of other attachments to include if they serve an important purpose:

- letters of support

- evaluation instruments

- articles or published material about the problem addressed in the proposal

- curriculum to be used in the program

- most recent annual report

- copy of a recent newsletter highlighting the organization's competence or staff achievements.

Don't substitute attachments for narrative. Don't shift information from the proposal narrative into the attachments section in an effort to circumvent page limits. Reviewers who don't find the proposal's narrative convincing won't turn to the attachments to learn more. Some reviewers, pressed for time, don't look at attachments at all.

Use standard-sized paper. Print all attachments on 8.5- by 11-inch paper so they can easily go through the auto-feed of a copier.

Keep attachments current. Old newsletters or newspaper clippings suggest that your organization has nothing more recent to show. Outdated letters of support make funders wonder if the authors still support your organization. Credibility suffers in both cases.

Consider support letters carefully. Because support letters provide endorsement rather than commitment, some funders have no interest in them. Attach support letters only when they can deepen the reader's understanding of the program, are written by someone who is essential to the program's success, or are requested by the funder. A letter from a client can demonstrate the value of your work in a way that nothing else can. A letter from an advocacy group can show that proposed beneficiaries support the program. Powerful support letters are specific. Vague or generic support letters are unconvincing and add pages without adding value.

It's okay for grant applicants to draft letters of support or to suggest language that supporters can use, but each letter must be unique. Boilerplate text, no matter how well written, suggests that support for the program is neither genuine nor enthusiastic.

When a letter from an influential group or individual makes an especially important point, excerpt the passage and use it in the main narrative with the note, "See attached letter."

Make them easy to find. If the number of attachments is stacking up, consider adding a table of contents.

Use pictures cautiously. A picture can reinforce the narrative. But it can also raise questions about confidentiality, unintentionally exploit clients, or take up space without adding value.

Don't add digital media unless asked. Attach these only if requested, funders seldom view or listen to them.

Give the feds their forms. Federal agencies generally require a variety of assurance and certification forms relating to issues such as the maintenance of a drug-free workplace, compliance with the Americans with Disabilities Act, use of funds for lobbying, etc. Be sure all required forms are signed and attached.

Submitting the Proposal

HARDCOPY SUBMISSIONS

Some funders still require that proposals be submitted in hard copy. When they do, here are some tips:

Understand the deadline. Some deadlines are the date by which your organization's package must be postmarked. Others are the date by which the document must be received. The difference between the two is critical. When funders impose deadlines, they're usually nonnegotiable, and a late proposal will be disqualified even if it's late by less than a minute.

Send it to the right address. Government funders often require that packages sent through the U.S. Postal Service be delivered to one address and that those sent via courier be delivered to another.

Check the receipt. Although it doesn't happen often, your organization may have to prove the proposal was sent by the deadline. Be sure the date and time are correct and legible on any receipt you receive from the post office or a courier service. Don't use your organization's mail meter. Because you can control the date on the meter, it's not valid proof of the mailing date.

Hand delivery? If you plan to hand-deliver your proposal, make sure that it's allowed and that you have a street address. You can't deliver to a post office box.

Government agencies are wary of deliveries, so you may not be able to drop off a package. Get a dated receipt for any package you deliver.

"Usually" isn't good enough. Don't count on an overnight delivery service to deliver overnight. They usually do, but it's a risk you should not take unless it's unavoidable.

Track it. Send the proposal package in a way that can be tracked. Then track it to make sure it's on its way to the correct destination. If it's not, you'll need to intervene.

Verify it. Confirm that the package was delivered and get the name of the person who signed for it. If you deliver it yourself, get a dated receipt to document that the funder received it.

ELECTRONIC SUBMISSIONS

Here are a few tips to help you with online submissions:

Register in advance. If your organization plans to submit proposals electronically to the federal government, register with Grants.gov now. Grants.gov is the only way to enter many federal grant competitions, and only registered users are allowed to submit proposals. Completing the registration process can take days, even longer if a problem arises.

Some other funders that require electronic submission of proposals may also require that you preregister to use their systems. Be on the lookout for this crucial detail and register early.

Check out the system. If your organization plans to submit electronically, visit the site ahead of time to get a sense of how it works. Try to determine whether it saves information or whether the entire application must be completed and submitted in one sitting. Make sure your organization's password has been activated. As soon as possible, conduct a test run to ensure system compatibility. Detect problems while there is still time to solve them.

Submit early. Some funders suggest submitting electronic proposals a few days before the deadline. That way, if applicants encounter technical problems, they'll have time to solve them. If you wait until the deadline, the funder's system may be overwhelmed by a crush of last-minute submissions and become erratic. The technical assistance team may be unable to respond to your email promptly. The help line may be continuously busy, or the voice mail may be full. No matter what, you must meet the deadline or be disqualified. Electronic submissions can be easy or maddening. Since you won't know which way it will go until you're in the middle of it, the only sensible approach is to plan for the worst, hope for the best, and submit early.

The help line. Though it may not always be able to save the day, keep the email address and telephone number of the funder's technical assistance line handy.

Control the format if you can. Some funders require applicants to upload proposals to a website. But when moving an electronic file from one system to another, formatting may become jumbled, making it difficult for the funder to decipher your documents. To avoid problems, keep the layout simple. Submit your files in PDF, if allowed, because this will lock the format.

Prepare for online forms. When the application is an online form, it requires thought and preparation just like any other proposal. Even when funders severely limit the number of words or characters you can use, don't be tempted to take a casual approach as though you were sending a quick email. It's best to print out the entire application, thoughtfully construct your responses offline, and then, when you're ready, complete the online form.

Some online applications require applicants to start all over if they fail to complete the task in one sitting. To avoid that trap, write the responses offline and then copy and paste them into the online form.

Keep a copy. Before hitting "submit," be sure you've saved a copy of everything.

Time zones. Pay attention to them. If the funder in Boston must receive the submission before 5 p.m. Eastern Time and it is being sent from California, the actual deadline is 2 p.m. Pacific Time.

Verify arrival. Clicking the "send" button doesn't guarantee that the electronic transmission went through. Verify that it arrived at the other end on time. If the system provides an automatic verification, print it out and file it. If it doesn't, call the funder and ask for verification. Be sure to record the name of the person who says it arrived.

Approval or Rejection— Now What?

Your organization may be awarded the requested grant, or it may not. Be prepared for the highs of acceptance or the lows of rejection. Try to accept either with grace and equanimity.

There is much to say about grant management and about building and maintaining relationships with funders, colleague organizations, and your community.

For now, here are a few brief words of advice.

IF THE GRANT PROPOSAL IS FULLY FUNDED

1. Thank the funder immediately and graciously.

2. Take time to celebrate with those who helped plan the program and prepare the proposal and those who committed support and resources.

3. Find out how the funder wants the grant to be acknowledged.

4. Read any documents the funder provides and review commitments made in your proposal. Be sure you know exactly what is expected.

5. Review the administrative requirements of the grant: funding draw-downs, reporting, record keeping, audits, site visits, etc. If the grant is a federal grant, get a copy of the agency's grant management policies and procedures. Also be sure that you, or another appropriate staff member, understand the requirements laid out in the grant administration circulars published by the Federal Office of Management and Budget.

6. Review the timeline for the project, update it as needed, and make sure it includes report due dates and anticipates other administrative requirements.

7. Provide the program director with a copy of the grant proposal and updated timeline and confirm that he or she understands record-keeping, administrative, and reporting requirements.

8. Make sure the program director knows which tasks require immediate attention: hiring/assigning staff, acquiring space, reviewing the evaluation plan with the evaluator, etc.

9. Get started! It's not uncommon for a grant recipient to fall three months behind at the beginning of a project. Your organization may be able to make up lost time later, but staying on schedule will make things easier in the long run.

IF THE GRANT PROPOSAL IS PARTIALLY FUNDED

1. Stay calm. Tell the funder how much your organization appreciates the partial grant award.

2. Ask the funder for time to review the budget and program design with your organization's managers and staff. Because the proposal assumed full funding, the reduced amount will probably mean revisions are in order.

3. Consider alternatives. Can the lost funding be replaced by engaging another funder? Must there be a reduction in the number of people served? Or the number of planned activities? Or the length of time the program will operate? How will all of this affect the projected outcomes?

4. Once your organization has decided how to proceed, discuss the revisions with the funder.

5. After reaching an agreement with the funder on how to proceed, submit changes to the proposal in writing and always ask the funder to respond in writing as well.

6. Then follow steps 2 through 9 as previously recommended when the grant proposal is fully funded.

IF THE GRANT PROPOSAL IS NOT FUNDED

1. Stay calm. This is not the end of the program or the careers of its planners. There will be other opportunities. Your job is to plan a strong program, prepare a competitive proposal, and submit it to an appropriate funder. No matter how well you do your job, your proposal won't always win.

2. Thank the funder for considering the proposal. If it's a private funder, ask for a meeting or phone call to discuss how the proposal might be improved. Neither request may be granted, but ask anyway. Your organization may have other opportunities to work with the funder, and even a rejection can lead to a long and productive relationship.

   If it's a government funder, ask to see the comments of those who reviewed the proposal. Try to discuss them with the staff person in charge of the grant program. Many proposals to federal agencies are funded the second time around, after changes have been made in response to reviewer comments.

3. After cooling off, look at the proposal with fresh eyes and consider carefully how it can be improved.

4. Call a meeting of your organization's program planning and proposal writing team to discuss the next steps. Be sure to involve partner organizations in the discussion so that you can all move forward together.

Take Care of Yourself & Never Give Up

We thank all of you who plan programs and write grant proposals. It's tough work. When you get tired, rest and rejuvenate yourself by visiting those who have benefitted from your effort. Never, never give up. The world would be a sadder and harder place without your work.

Adapting

The Grantsmanship Center Model for

Arts & Culture Proposals

Arts and culture approaches are often used as methods for accomplishing a range of economic, social, and educational outcomes. Grant proposals to support that work should follow The Grantsmanship Center Model laid out in this book.

But proposals to support artistic or cultural pursuits for their own sake—because opera enlivens the world or the sculpture garden expands our perceptions—are somewhat different.

The fit between the proposal and the potential funder is always critical, and never more so than when seeking support for purely artistic and cultural pursuits. It doesn't matter how exciting the play will be if the funder receiving your proposal is interested only in health care. For a proposal to be successful, the importance of art and culture in society, in private lives, and in the community must be a mutually held value.

In this type of proposal, only the Problem and Outcomes Sections of the model require adaptation.

Problem

Describe the value and benefits of the artistic or cultural pursuit and tell the reader how it enriches the community. If the population you will serve is not now enjoying those benefits, explain why. Do they have to travel too far? Is admission too expensive? Are there language, cultural, or physical barriers? Document the barriers and be sure to address them in the Methods Section.

Program Outcomes

Outcomes will focus on the number of people served, an increase in the number served, and participant's perceived benefits or expanded perceptions.

- *5,000 people will attend the symphony's community concert.*

- *Within 12 months, the number of third-grade students who participate in artist-led tours and activities will increase by 50%, from 200 to 300.*

- *Of the 200 people who participate in exhibit-related lectures and films, 170 (85%) will express enjoyment of the events, interest in attending future events, and expanded understanding of modern art.*

- *Of the 150 people who attend the interfaith discussion group, 143 (95%) will report a deeper understanding of and tolerance for belief systems other than their own.*

In addition to the usual attachments, arts and culture proposals often provide evidence of past accomplishment—a CD of the orchestra's performance, quality photos of paintings, etc.

— Based on an article by Judith M. Gooch
Trainer Emeritus, *The Grantsmanship Center*

Adapting The Grantsmanship Center Model for
Capacity-Building Proposals

Proposal writers may be aware that funders support capacity building but are often unsure of what fits into that category. Although proposal writers may be confused about the definition, funders aren't—they're amazingly consistent in what they define as capacity building and what they don't.

To funders, capacity building is about strengthening organizational infrastructure, management systems, and governance. It is not about program development or expansion or a capital project such as a new facility. Examples of activities appropriate for capacity-building grants include:

- Assessment of the organization's management and governance systems

- Evaluation of service effectiveness

- Strategic planning

- Board or staff development to achieve well-defined governance or management outcomes

- Fund development planning

- Establishment of a fund development program

- Succession planning

- Mergers or other restructuring

- Technology upgrades

- Establishment of a volunteer management system

- External communications strategies

When preparing a capacity-building proposal, write from a position of strength. Help the funder understand why an investment in the infrastructure of the organization will pay off in terms of services to its constituents and progress toward its mission.

Funders generally make capacity-building grants to organizations they know and trust, those with which they have established relationships. These grants are for making good organizations better. That's very different from capacity repair! If your board and administrators have been asleep at the switch, funders are unlikely to make the investment.

A few sections of The Grantsmanship Center Model will need to be adapted for a capacity-building proposal.

Introduction to the Applicant Organization

Because capacity building is about improving your agency's ability to fulfill its mission and deliver services, this section sets the stage for the request. Discuss the target population the organization serves, demonstrate a track record of accomplishment, and emphasize benefits to the community. Discuss changes and improvements in management and governance that are already in place. Demonstrate that the organization's board and executive staff take organizational improvement seriously.

Problem

Because capacity-building proposals focus on addressing organizational needs, it's critical to discuss those needs as an opportunity for continued improvement and strengthening.

Perhaps the fiscal system needs updating because of new government grants that require more rigorous procedures. Maybe the board needs training because it has expanded to include new members.

Updated organizational assessment and strategic plans are benchmarks of strong organizations; explain that the need to update these documents is based on the organization's commitment to continuous improvement. The organization may also need to update these documents because it is at a point of critical growth or change.

Sometimes infrastructure needs to be updated just to keep pace with the expected standards of modern business practice, and that's fine. But if the proposal shows that the need has resulted from lapses in planning, management failures, or audit findings that require corrective actions, you'll end up with what The Grantsmanship Center calls a "self-indicting proposal," one that inadvertently raises questions about your organization's competence and credibility.

The strongest capacity-building proposals are based on an organizational assessment. Most community foundations and United Ways can recommend good tools for this process. Hospitals, educational institutions, and other organizations that undergo regular certification reviews can usually use information from those assessments.

Because the governing body and executive staff are responsible for policy and management, they are the ones who must conduct the assessment and develop the improvement plan.

All capacity-building proposals must describe how the targeted need was identified, explain why addressing it is important at this particular time, and demonstrate that the board is involved and committed to the effort.

Outcomes

Outcomes for capacity-building grants won't be direct client outcomes. Instead, capacity-building outcomes will be products that will contribute to better client outcomes. Here are a few examples:

- *By May 31, 2015, the board of directors will vote to approve the Family Center's new 5-year strategic plan that will guide the organization's services and growth and contribute to improved outcomes for clients.*

- *By May 31, 2015, the database will be complete and installed, and identified staff will be trained in its operation. By June 30, 2015, monthly data reports will be provided to administrators and program managers to guide resource allocation and decision-making.*

- *By May 31, 2015, the new volunteer management system will be fully operational and will result in reports of increased satisfaction by both volunteers and clients.*

You may expect such products as a strategic plan, fund development plan, or marketing plan to contribute to stronger programs and services. You may be able to detail how a new accounting system will enhance service management. Or you may expect a new volunteer management system to result in an increased number of volunteers that will expand services. When describing the product to be developed with grant funding, relate it to long-term benefits to clients.

Methods

This section will provide details on the product that will result from the grant and how it will be produced. For a new IT system, for example, you'll describe the hardware and software that will be used, why it was selected, when it will be purchased and installed, how staff will be trained to use it, how it will be maintained, and how the organization will keep it updated.

For a strategic plan, you'll lay out a timeline of tasks showing when they'll be accomplished and who'll be responsible for them. You'll describe the issues to be addressed by the plan, when it will be completed and how the plan will be used.

Demonstrate that staff members or consultants who'll be leading the project, or who will play critical roles, are well qualified. And lay out the chain of command: Who will supervise staff members or consultants?

Evaluation

Explain how the organization will assess whether system or infrastructure improvements are effective. And when possible, plan to assess the improvement's impact on clients. Financial statements might, for example, indicate that the new fund development plan is producing increased income and might also document that the income has been applied directly to improve client services. Or you may be able to show that the new volunteer system has resulted in more volunteers who are providing increased services to clients.

It will be harder to show how a new organizational assessment or strategic plan is having a direct impact on clients. But in addition to having a quality product in hand by the expected time, the Evaluation Section can note services that have been identified for improvement or expansion or note future client benefits supported by the plan.

Future Support

If the organization will hire new staff, explain how it will continue to pay those salaries and related expenses. If the organization will purchase new technology or equipment, explain how it will pay for ongoing operation, maintenance, and upgrades.

Some foundations ask for a business plan covering several years, especially if costs are high. Even if they don't require a formal plan, show that the organization has given consideration to future costs and that the governing body is committed to meeting costs associated with the funder's initial grant investment.

— Based on an article by Susan Chandler
Trainer Emeritus, *The Grantsmanship Center*

Adapting The Grantsmanship Center Model for
Capital Project Proposals

Capital projects generally require funding from several sources and deal with major facility renovation, purchasing or building a facility, or purchasing major equipment. Purchase of small equipment and building repairs do not fit in this category. The Grantsmanship Center Model requires some adaptation for capital proposals.

Introduction to the Applicant Organization

In addition to standard elements included in The Grantsmanship Center Model, the Introduction Section should provide fairly extensive detail about the issue the organization addresses, including the target population and demographics.

Problem

Explain the situation that requires capital investment. Has the organization grown so that the facility is no longer adequate? Does limited space impact its ability to provide services? If so, how are services limited? Must health, safety, or zoning requirements be addressed? Are there opportunities for the organization to do more or better work?

Is the equipment critical for delivering state-of-the-art services and achieving positive client outcomes?

Methods

Cover these three specific areas in the Methods Section:

1. **Describe why the option selected is the best choice.** What other options were considered and why weren't they chosen? Show that the planning and consideration were thorough.

2. **Describe the facility or equipment.** How big will the facility be? What's the layout? How will it be used? Who are the architects and engineers? Do you have the required permits? In addition to a construction timeline, you will generally be expected to have an identified site and completed architectural plans which, are usually attached to the proposal.

   For major equipment, provide detailed information on make, model, capacity, required staff training, maintenance expectations, and future upgrade needs.

3. **Describe the fundraising plan and include a timeline.** Identify the constituencies you expect to contribute to the effort, how much you expect to raise from each, and why the plan is realistic. Describe the fundraising structure: Who will do the asking? Are there committees? What are their roles and responsibilities?

   Leadership gifts should be secured *first*, before the campaign goes public and before grant proposals are submitted. These gifts come from those with the biggest commitment to the organization and might come from board members, staff, long-time supporters, or advisory committee members.

   Many grantmakers require a narrative for each constituency in the plan explaining why each funding goal is realistic and how the fundraising work will be completed. Some grantmakers require a completed feasibility study, an assessment of the community's ability to donate the expected amounts.

   Summarize your income expectations in a table. An example is shown on the next page.

Constituency	Campaign Goal	Committed	To Be Raised
Leadership gift	100,000	100,000	0
Major donors ($10,000+)	150,000	97,000	53,000
Individuals ($1,000–$10,000)	75,000	12,000	63,000
Approved mortgage	500,000	500,000	0
Donated architect & engineer fees	75,000	75,000	0
Community fundraisers	10,000	0	10,000
Foundations:			
Red Foundation	150,000		150,000
Blue Foundation	100,000	100,000	
Green Foundation	50,000		50,000
Yellow Foundation	30,000	30,000	
Purple Foundation	25,000	25,000	
Corporate support	90,000	30,000	60,000
TOTALS	**$1,355,000**	**$969,000**	**$386,000**

Outcomes

Capital project proposals generally include process objectives—measurable, quantifiable statements of activity—rather than the sort of program outcomes described in The Grantsmanship Center Model. So capital project outcomes will relate to completing fundraising on time; to completing facilities on time and within budget; or to purchasing and installing equipment and training staff according to the timeline laid out in the Methods Section.

The Outcomes Section should also specify how you expect the new facility or equipment to improve or expand services. This will be framed in terms of measurable increases in services provided, decreases in waiting lists, and the like.

Evaluation

Identify the person responsible for monitoring fundraising and construction or equipment purchase and installation. Explain how plans will be modified if needed. And include plans to assess long-term impact on services, showing how you will track increases or improvements.

Future Support

Once the project is complete, how will your organization support additional operating expenses? Additional expenses might include: staff; higher utility, insurance, or maintenance costs; or ongoing equipment upgrades.

For facilities, many funders require a 3-to-5-year business plan detailing the increased costs that will result and how the organization will cover them. Even when the funder doesn't require a plan, you've got to have one, and this is where you'll describe it in the proposal.

Budget

Break the budget into major categories and make sure it matches your fundraising plan; the fundraising plan shows revenues, and the budget shows expenses. For facilities, major categories might include land, fees and permits, professional fees, construction, furnishings, site preparation, etc. For equipment, major categories might include the equipment itself, site preparation, installation, and staff training.

You may be asked to provide detailed bids at some point in the grant review process.

— Based on an article by Susan Chandler
Trainer Emeritus, *The Grantsmanship Center*

Adapting The Grantsmanship Center Model for
General Operating Proposals

Grants to support general operations come almost exclusively from foundations and corporations, rarely from government sources. They're similar to gifts from individual donors because they recognize the organization's overall value to the community, and the funder understands that the organization will continue to request general operating support in the future. Funders generally provide operating grants only to organizations with which they have an established relationship.

An operating proposal includes the same categories of information presented in The Grantsmanship Center Model, with some adjustments. Rather than describing what the organization will do in the future, an operating proposal focuses on what the organization is now doing, how it is currently making a difference.

If the request is in the form of a short letter, omit the section headings. Otherwise, customize the headings. Rather than *Introduction to the Applicant Organization*, for example, you might substitute *The Sweetwater Family Center: Serving the Community Since 1980*. Rather than *Methods*, you might substitute *Description of Family Center Services*.

Proposal Section	Adaptation for General Operating Proposals
Summary	Ask for a specific amount, and tell the reader how the requested grant will contribute to the organization's total budget for the upcoming year.
Introduction to Applicant	Provide only a brief history of the organization and describe its mission.
Problem	Describe and document the issues the organization addresses in pursuit of its mission. Be sure to describe the target population.
Outcomes	Tell the reader how the organization is making a difference in the issues it addresses. Describe the outcomes it is now producing. The operating grant is seeking support to help the organization continue to produce the same high-quality results.
Methods	Tell the reader about the organization's current programs and services. Be sure to include the number of people served. An operating proposal invites the funder to support this work.
Evaluation	Explain the type of data the organization collects, how it monitors its work, how it measures service outcomes, and its commitment to continuous improvement. Describe service and outcome reports that the organization will provide to the funder.
Future Support	Stress the organization's strong financial history and assure the donor that most of the operating funds for the coming year are in place from other sources. Name a few (i.e., program income, individual donors, events, other grants). Remember, funders are looking for strong partners. Send the message that, in spite of a sound funding base, your organization needs additional or continued funding to ensure that clients will continue to receive the full benefit of your organization's services.
Budget	The budget for an operating proposal is your organization's annual budget. Include a clear document showing the major categories of expense.

Adapting The Grantsmanship Center Model for
Planning Proposals

Recognizing the crucial role of planning in large-scale community projects, some funders offer planning grants. This type of grant results in a broadly accepted community plan of action. Some funders require grant seekers to successfully complete a formal community planning process before they compete for an implementation grant.

Planning grants and implementation grants produce different types of results. A *planning* grant results in a product, a plan of action. An *implementation* grant results in a change in the problem itself. An implementation grant is the same thing as a program grant and follows the basic Grantsmanship Center Model.

Although developing a proposal for a planning grant is much the same as developing a request for a program grant, there are a few important differences. Here are the most critical sections of a grant proposal in terms of these differences.

PROBLEM

Planning Proposal
The Problem Section offers solid, well-supported evidence of the problem in the target service area. If the target area is one neighborhood in a large urban area, citywide or countywide data isn't good enough. You'll need neighborhood or ZIP-code specific information.

Once you've defined and documented the problem and its significance, you'll explain the causes of the situation. Hard data from research findings, statistics, and reviews of professional literature will be critical, but the perspectives of community groups will also weigh heavily in the discussion.

Program Proposal
The discussion of the problem is the same as that of a planning proposal. If your organization has completed a community planning process prior to development of the program proposal, you'll have a great wealth of anecdotal information to add to the hard data you'll present. If there has not been a community planning process, the voices of community members will still be present, but are unlikely to be as strong.

OUTCOMES

Planning Proposal
The long-term goal of a planning grant is a reduction in the problem. But the specific outcome to be produced by a planning grant during the project period will be a product, a plan of action. The plan should be well-reasoned, broadly accepted, and designed to address factors that are causing the problem. To the greatest extent possible, the plan should be based on solid evidence that the approaches identified are likely to succeed.

Here's an example of a proposed outcome for a planning grant:

> *Within eight months, an action plan will be adopted by the community coalition:*
>
> *(a) The action plan will be based on research or other evidence that the proposed approaches are likely to be effective in addressing the problem.*
>
> *(b) Process documents will verify that the eight targeted segments of the community were vigorously engaged in data gathering, research, and planning.*

Program Proposal

The long-term goal of an implementation grant is also a reduction in the problem. But the proposed outcomes will be specific, measurable changes in the problem or in factors causing the problem. These changes will take place during the period of grant funding. Here are examples of outcomes for a program to address poverty:

> *(a) By the end of the five-year implementation period, 200 new long-term, full-time jobs paying above minimum wage will be in place in the target community.*
>
> *(b) By the end of the five-year implementation period, the unemployment rate in the target community will have dropped from the current average of 25% to an average of 15%.*

METHODS

Planning Proposal

The Methods Section provides a detailed blueprint of how you'll conduct the planning process. Who will lead the charge? Who has agreed to participate? What's the timeline? What are the specific questions the process will address? What community resources is your group bringing to the table: meeting space, social media, reporting? Will you bring in experts to discuss the data or to help explore the most promising approaches for addressing the problem?

Program Proposal

For an implementation proposal, the Methods Section provides a detailed description of exactly what the community will do to address the problem. It tells the reader specifically what the action plan is and how it will be implemented. You'll lay out the major components of activity and describe who will do what, and when and how they'll do it. You'll describe the roles and responsibilities of the various groups involved and the resources the community is providing for the effort.

EVALUATION

It's important to gather and assess evaluation information as a project is rolling out. This provides valuable information that can lead to changes in a process that isn't working or may prompt course corrections when the program isn't producing the intended outcomes. Evaluation data should contribute to continuous improvement, so don't wait until the end of the grant period to determine whether your process or program worked. That's too late.

Planning Proposal

The Evaluation Section describes how you'll track and document the planning process and its results. You'll list the questions to be answered and tell the reader how you'll gather needed information. Here are some examples of questions that may be included:

• Are intended groups participating?

• What evidence-based approaches are being explored?

• Are identified questions being answered?

• Is the timeline being followed?

• Has a plan been produced on time?

• Is the plan broadly supported by the community?

• Have there been unexpected challenges?

To gather the needed information, you might examine minutes of meetings, conduct and analyze surveys of planning participants and other community members, or reference interim reports and presentation notes.

Program Proposal

The Evaluation Section of a program proposal includes two components:

• *Process evaluation.* This component describes how you'll assess whether the program is being implemented as planned and working as expected. It describes how you'll know the degree to which the

program is following the established action plan. It tells how you'll note successes and challenges, how you'll document whether the intended people are engaged, and whether the expected resources have materialized, etc.

• *Outcome evaluation.* This component describes how you'll know the degree to which the proposed outcomes are being achieved. It tells how you'll produce, tally, and analyze specific data. The information that will be produced by this component of the evaluation will tell you, the funder, and the community how effectively the program is addressing the problem.

BUDGET

The Budget Section defines the resources required to complete a planning process or to implement a program. It provides detail on in-kind resources that will be used; cash that will be provided by partner organizations or other funders; and line items that will be supported by the requested grant funds and the other resources.

Planning Proposal

What resources does a planning process require? Typically, staff and volunteer time are required for coordination, logistics, administration, and clerical tasks. Consultants may be needed for facilitation or expert testimony. Meetings may require conference rooms and auditoriums. Making it all happen will probably require communications, printing, supplies, surveys, and more.

Program Proposal

Implementing a program usually costs far more than planning it. The resources required will depend on the various activities to be implemented and will probably include such line items as staffing, training, supervision, office space, transportation and travel, supplies, equipment, curriculum, and evaluation costs.

In a broad-based community effort, it's also likely that a number of community partners will be involved in program implementation, and more than one organization will receive a portion of the requested grant funds.

Adapting The Grantsmanship Center Model for
Research Proposals

Program proposals seek funds to directly confront a problem, meet a need, or enhance the quality of life in a specific location, for a specific population. Research proposals, on the other hand, seek funds to answer questions. The answers the research provides are meant to create new knowledge and benefit society as a whole.

While program and research proposals have some common elements, there are major differences. Here's a section-by-section look at how a research proposal differs from a program proposal.

Program Proposal	Research Proposal
Summary Brief overview of entire proposal. Prepares the reader to comprehend the narrative.	**Abstract or Project Summary** Brief overview of entire proposal. Often used to assign the proposal to a specific review group.

Program Proposal	Research Proposal
Introduction to Applicant Organization Focus is on demonstrating the credibility of the organization that will operate the program: mission and history, programs and services, community and populations served, history of producing positive results, partnerships and collaborations, expertise in program topic.	**Qualifications of Principal Investigator and Team** Focus is on the quality and experience of the investigator who will lead the research and on the team of researchers who will be involved: research accomplishments to date, contributions to knowledge in specific research area, professional stature, relevant publications.
Present Knowledge/Literature Review Understanding current knowledge in the topic area is essential to understanding the problem, and to planning a relevant, effective program. While program proposals seldom include a formal literature review or a separate section for discussion of present knowledge, it's expected that this information will be folded into the Problem Section and the Methods Section.	**Present Knowledge/Literature Review** To provide a context for the project, proposals include a review of the most recent and pertinent research in the field. A survey of the literature (almost always from peer-reviewed publications) ensures that the project has been formulated with an understanding of relevant precedents and that the project will not address questions that have already been satisfactorily answered. The literature review is usually included as a separate section of the proposal.
Problem Describes and documents the situation that is causing concern and motivating the grant proposal. Explains the situation's significance and its causes.	**Research Question** Defines the question to be answered.
Outcomes Defines specific positive changes in the situation that are expected to result from the proposed program.	**Significance of Question** Describes why the question is relevant—why answering it is worth the investment.

Program Proposal	Research Proposal
Methods Defines activities the applicant will use to achieve the desired outcomes. Includes a timeline. Describes roles and responsibilities of collaborators.	**Methods** Describes: research approach, experimental methods and procedures, how results will be analyzed, how investigator's institution or organization will support the research.
Resources A description of the resources to be used in the program is included in the Methods Section.	**Resources** Applicants must document the equipment and other resources available to carry out the research. For social science or clinical science projects, this may include the availability of an adequate number of appropriate subjects to study. The applicant must also document that institutional safeguards are in place, such as protocols on the use of human subjects or vertebrate animals. Often the grant proposal must be accompanied by a letter of commitment from the institution, assuring the funder that these resources are, in fact, available to the researcher.
Evaluation Describes the process the applicant will use to determine whether outcomes are being achieved and whether the program is being implemented as planned.	**Evaluation** In general, these proposals don't require evaluation sections. In research, evaluation is carried out by peer-reviewed publication of research results. But there are exceptions. Some proposals may require data analysis or evaluation depending on application guidelines or type of research.
Future Support Describes how the applicant will continue the program or its impact once grant funding ends.	**Future Plans and Dissemination** Proposals include a discussion of how the research will lead to further investigation that will continue to advance understanding in the field. This may be a separate section or woven into discussion of the research question or its significance. Proposals often include a section describing how research findings will be disseminated (i.e., journal articles, conferences, workshops for teachers, programs for undergraduates, data sharing).

Program Proposal	Research Proposal
Budget Delineates income and expenses of program implementation.	**Budget** Delineates income and expenses of completing the research.
Budget Justification Describes and justifies expenses: why each is necessary; how each was calculated (if not included in the line-item budget).	**Budget Justification** Describes and justifies expenses: why each is necessary; how each was calculated (if not included in the line-item budget).

The Language of Research Proposals

Because most research proposals are highly technical, proposal writers may feel compelled to use dense, complex language. That's a mistake in any sort of grant proposal. Guidelines for research proposals also emphasize the need for clear, direct language. The initial reviewers of a research proposal may be generalists rather than experts in a specific sub-specialty and they are likely to be put off by or to misunderstand inflated or needlessly complex language. Overblown language makes the proposal more difficult to read and to evaluate fairly.

It's especially critical that abstracts be understandable to a non-specialist. The National Science Foundation asks that abstracts be directed to a "scientifically literate lay reader." Because the reviewers for a research proposal are often chosen based on the proposal title and a preliminary reading of the abstract, it's imperative that the non-specialist grasp the full implications of the proposal right away. Otherwise, the proposal could be sent to the wrong people for review.

The statement of significance must also be understood by a broader audience. In some review processes, panelists read only the title, abstract, and significance statements. They then consider the in-depth review by one or two experts in the specialty area of the proposal. If the title, abstract, and significance statements are not immediately clear to the entire panel, the proposal will have trouble winning support.

THE GRANTSMANSHIP CENTER

Get funding. Create change.

Afterword

I first read *Program Planning & Proposal Writing* as a homework assignment when being trained by its author, Norton Kiritz. This book transformed deadly dry material into laugh out-loud stories, cementing new concepts into my brain—easy, smart and full of humor and heart. I thought that whoever wrote such a book must be special.

That was 30 some years ago and the beginning of my life with Norton Kiritz and *Program Planning & Proposal Writing*. About a year later Norton and I were married. It's his book that first stole my heart. It wasn't intimidating and it was fun to read. Most people would rather have dental work done than read a book about grants. This book was the exception—revolutionary in both content and style.

By the year 2000, *Program Planning & Proposal Writing* had sold more than a million copies. Bought by people in hundreds of thousands of organizations so they could help millions more. Used by universities, government offices, and uncounted nonprofits, translated into three languages, with documented use in 43 countries. Every day we get orders for the original *Program Planning & Proposal Writing* because the core concepts are classic and universal—still relevant after 40 years. This modest 47-page book has had huge and lasting impact.

But the world of grants has evolved, and even this classic needed an update. Norton died in 2006 before he could produce this next edition. I'm forever grateful to Barbara Floersch—the brains and the source of experience and knowledge who bravely stepped into Norton's shoes.

Fifteen years ago, as an experienced grant proposal writer but a new trainer, Barbara peppered Norton with questions that started with "Norton, tell me about…." And then she listened. Norton talked about what he loved most—helping people build effective programs by cleaning up their logic, challenging their assumptions, and giving them guidance about writing good proposals. Barbara soaked it all up, making that knowledge and wisdom part of her own training for the Center.

I don't think anybody else could have successfully updated this book. No other colleague has been so flat-out uncompromising and so gripped with getting it right. No ego. Driven to capture the truth in the clearest way possible. Barbara's insight and knowledge are exceeded only by her tenacity and compassion. And few people loved Norton and this work more.

Thanks to Barbara, this book contains the most up-to-date information as well as new material which complements the original.

My job was to keep clutter out and Norton in. My mantra was "access." I stood in the reader's shoes asking over and over, "What *exactly* do you mean?" The challenge was to take readers cover to cover easily, deliver maximum information and retain the substance and humor of Norton's original work. We saved every scrap of the original that we could because Norton's deep and extraordinary voice is irreplaceable.

One last thing. Long ago, Norton corrected me when I used the term "grant writer." He explained: If you award grants, then you're a "grant writer." But if you want to get grants, then you're not a "grant writer," you're a grant seeker, or a grant proposal writer.

We debated raising this issue because it can be a sensitive subject. Some of the most eager, engaged, hard-working and productive people use the title "grant writer." So, this distinction may seem like caviling, or worse, criticism. But if you want language that hits the mark, "grant writer" doesn't do justice to the job. If one actually means "grant proposal writer," then "grant writer" shortchanges. It leaves a gap. And in that void, there's room for confusion and misunderstanding. Developing a successful proposal is much more than writing.

"Grant writer" implies that people get grants just by putting words on a page—like pulling a rabbit out of a hat. But more troubling, "grant writer" puts the focus on the money—the grant. What matters much more than the money is what your program will accomplish—the results—the outcomes you're proposing to achieve. Sure, money is part of the process, but it's just not the most important part.

Successful grant proposal development relies on solid program planning, research, and teamwork. It's the result of understanding the community, its needs and the causes of the problems. It's a thoughtful process, which at its best is logical, culturally inclusive and inspired by a drive to help others.

Whatever your title—proposal writer, program planner, development director, executive director, grant professional, board member, volunteer, grant writer or something else—we honor and applaud you for what you accomplish every day, knowing that you work long and hard to secure funding for essential work in your community. We wish you the greatest of success and hope this book will become a trusted companion on your journey.

— CATHLEEN E. KIRITZ

President, *The Grantsmanship Center*

Index

About Norton J. Kiritz

Some people break out of the ordinary, take risks, learn new rules, struggle with obstacles, and create something lasting. Norton Kiritz did, and he empowered hundreds of thousands of nonprofits to take the same journey. He wrote *Program Planning & Proposal Writing* in 1972, and it became the spirit and spine of the movement he triggered.

Norton's signature was a relentless creativity: seeing a problem and taking action to deal with it. His engineering major at Cornell didn't let him get close enough to people, so he switched to psychology at UCLA. He lost his dog, saw the need for a service to track wandering pets, and started a business. No good camp options for his son? He started a summer camp.

His talent for solving problems led to a role in the War on Poverty. As a planner for the Los Angeles Community Action Agency, he saw neighborhood nonprofits struggling to make a dent in discrimination, poor nutrition, substandard housing, and more. Good people were trying to help good people, but they were frustrated by their inexperience with funding guidelines and deadlines, by long lines at the funders' doors, and by the challenges of trying to build and manage solid programs.

So Norton Kiritz launched The Grantsmanship Center to revolutionize the system, and he wrote *Program Planning & Proposal Writing* as an operating manual for all who would join his new adventure. Some people thought—maybe some still do—it would be enough to teach nonprofits to "get the words right," then money would flow. Norton knew better.

He wanted to help nonprofits get the work right, and he dedicated his enterprise to that purpose. Norton inspired a corps of trainers to follow his lead, to challenge assumptions, to insist on clear thinking and clear writing. He pushed grant seekers to understand funding sources and to avoid the beggar's slouch. He was tough on funders too, urging them to be more transparent, more consistent, and more available to answer questions and facilitate the flow of money to worthwhile projects.

Norton Kiritz worked for 34 years to define and strengthen grantsmanship. He guided trainers, designed new programs, and nurtured the movement until he died in 2006. Hundreds of thousands of nonprofits he reached built relationships with funders and communities and got the funding needed for their work. His training programs and publications have improved the odds so that good people can help more good people.

Grantsmanship. It's in your hands.

Grantsmanship done right is a powerful tool that brings a bounty of good into our communities: improved health, support and sustenance to those who are struggling, vibrant arts and cultural offerings to connect us, research that expands our minds, and energy that expands our hearts.

With this book, we welcome you to The Grantsmanship Center's 50-year tradition of inspiring, teaching, and supporting community champions who use grants for building a better world.

Check out tgci.com for more resources to help you move forward. Our offerings include the following training and services:

- *Grantsmanship Training Program*
- *Competing for Federal Grants*
- *Essential Grant Skills*
- *Research Proposal Workshop*
- *Grant Management Essentials*
- *Designing Programs for Results*
- *Proposal Review Tools*
- Live and on-demand webinars
- Help creating grant applications
- Consultation and coaching
- Speaking engagements
- Quality publications
- Specialized training in response to organizational needs and/or specific grant competitions and guidelines.

We love to hear from you! Let us know if you have a question, an idea, or want to tell us what you think about this book. Email: info@tgci.com.

Join us and more than 145,000 alumni working for a more brilliant and equitable world.